LAW ENFORCEMENT
FUNERAL MANUAL

ABOUT THE AUTHOR

William P. Sanders is a United Methodist Pastor. He has earned a Bachelor and a Master of Science degree, a Master of Divinity degree, and a Doctor of Ministry degree. Chaplain Sanders is a member of the International Conference of Police Chaplains, the Association of Traumatic Stress Specialists, and the International Critical Incident Stress Foundation. He is a Certified Master Chaplain (CMC) by the International Conference of Police Chaplains, a Certified Trauma Responder (CTR) by the Association of Traumatic Stress Specialists, and is trained in Critical Incident Stress Management. Chaplain Sanders was a former police officer with the City of Costa Mesa, California and currently serves as a volunteer chaplain for the Michigan State Police.

The International Conference of Police Chaplains

Second Edition

LAW ENFORCEMENT FUNERAL MANUAL

A Practical Guide for Law Enforcement
Agencies When Faced With the Death of a
Member of Their Department

By

Chaplain William P. Sanders, Author and Compiler
Certified Master Chaplain, I.C.P.C.

CHARLES C THOMAS • PUBLISHER, LTD.
Springfield • Illinois • U.S.A.

Published and Distributed Throughout the World by

CHARLES C THOMAS • PUBLISHER, LTD.
2600 South First Street
Springfield, Illinois 62704

© 2006 by CHARLES C THOMAS • PUBLISHER, LTD.

ISBN 0-398-07660-X (spiral)

Library of Congress Catalog Card Number: 2006044463

With THOMAS BOOKS *careful attention is given to all details of manufacturing
and design. It is the Publisher's desire to present books that are satisfactory as to their
physical qualities and artistic possibilities and appropriate for their particular use.*
THOMAS BOOKS *will be true to those laws of quality that assure a good name
and good will.*

Printed in the United States of America
SM-R-3

Library of Congress Cataloging-in-Publication Data
Sanders, William P., Chaplain.
  Law enforcement funeral manual : a practical guide for law enforcement
agencies when faced with the death of a member of their department /
William P. Sanders. -- 2nd ed.
      p. cm.
  At head of title: The International Conference of Police Chaplains.
  Includes bibliographical references and index.
  ISBN 0-398-07660-X (spiral : alk. paper)
  1. Police--United States--Handbooks, manuals, etc. 2. Funeral rites and
ceremonies--United States--Handbooks, manuals, etc. 3. Chaplains,
Police--United States--Handbooks, manuals, etc. I. International Conference
of Police Chaplains. II. Title.
  HV7936.F85S26 2006
  393.088'3632--dc22   2006044463

Dedicated in loving memory of
Chaplain John A. "Jack" Price
August 4, 1928 – May 4, 1998

Ordained Lutheran Minister (37 years)

Chaplain–Albuquerque, New Mexico Police Department 1969-1998

Co-Founder and second President of
the International Conference of Police Chaplains.

The annual International Conference of Police Chaplains Awards
for Excellence in Chaplaincy are named in his honor.

In 1982 he was given the Distinguished Citizen of New Mexico Award.

On July 8, 1998, the main headquarters buildings of the
Albuquerque Police Department and the Bernalillo County Sheriff's
Department was named the "John A. Price Law Enforcement Center."

The International Conference of Police Chaplains (ICPC) is an organization that supports volunteer and paid law enforcement chaplains. It helps law enforcement agencies develop chaplaincy programs or improve their chaplaincy programs. The ICPC provides its members with educational opportunities in training seminars and materials and a network of mutual support helps disseminate and share information about law enforcement chaplaincy.

The International Conference of Police Chaplains was founded in 1973. It is ecumenical and a non-profit organization. The ICPC has over 2,700 active members in all 50 states of the United States of America, 7 provinces of Canada, and in 10 other countries. Its logo appears above and on the cover of this manual.

To contact the International Conference of Police Chaplains: office address: P.O. Box 5590, Destin, Florida 32540; office telephones: (850) 654-9736, FAX (850) 654-9742; E-mail: icpc@gnt.net, Web-site: www.icpc4cops.org.

INTRODUCTION AND ACKNOWLEDGMENTS

This funeral manual is intended to provide law enforcement agencies with a quick and informative reference when the unthinkable occurs—an unexpected death of a departmental member. The material contained herein has been gathered by the International Conference of Police Chaplains from numerous departments and sources. The author has utilized these materials and others that he has gathered. Credit is given when materials were cited or adapted.

The task of writing/composing a funeral manual that will cover all law enforcement circumstances/protocols and religious beliefs is very difficult. The following information is offered as a suggestion and a beginning place. This information will likely need to be adapted/adjusted to the philosophy/theology of those who suffered the loss of their loved one and the departments they served.

Included in this manual is information about survivor resources, helps and support agencies. Particular attention should be given to Laurie Erickson's suggestions of ongoing care for the deceased member's family. These will be found in the sections entitled: "Taking Care of Our Own" and "Promoting Healthy Healing" (Chapter 6, pages 61–65). Mrs. Erickson offers these suggestions from her own personal experience. Mrs. Erickson's husband, Michigan State Trooper Byron J. Erickson, died in the line of duty on July 31, 1993.

Special appreciation is given to Chief Brian Russell of the Buchanan Police Department, Michigan, for allowing his department's "Line of Duty or Serious Injury" General Order to be included in this manual as an example for other departments/agencies to use in drafting their own policies and procedures (see Appendix A, pages 79–102). Also, thanks to the Mt. Vernon Police Department, Illinois, for being able to use their Line of Duty Injury or Death Information form (see pages 71–76).

The author thanks the following chaplains and persons who read this manual and perfected it (listed in alphabetical order): Rev. Dr. Paul Blacketor, Keene Police Department, Keene, New Hampshire; Mr. Mano Brahmbhatt, P.T.; Rev. David DeRevere, Executive Director, International Conference of Police Chaplains; Rev. Harold Elliott, Arlington Police Department, Arlington, Texas; Rev. Murray Fricke, Cheyenne Police Department, Cheyenne, Wyoming; Rev. Andrew Jackson, Michigan State Police; Rev. Anwar Khalifa, Tyler Police Department, Tyler, Texas; The Rev. Ronald Kobata, Maui Police Department, Maui, Hawaii; Rev. Dan Lovin, Jefferson County Sheriff's Office, Mt. Vernon, Illinois; Rabbi Dr. Stephen Passamaneck, Bureau of Alcohol, Tobacco and Firearms, Sherman Oaks, California; Sister Ann Stamm, Livonia Police Department, Livonia, Michigan and Rev. Bernard White, Skokie Police Department, Skokie, Illinois.

CONTENTS

Page

Introduction and Acknowledgments ix

Chapter

SECTION I–WHERE DO WE START?

1. PREPARING FOR THE FUNERAL 5
   Death Notifications 5
   The Role of the Chaplain in Departmental Funerals 7

SECTION II–ELEMENTS
OF THE LAW ENFORCEMENT FUNERAL

2. BASIC ELEMENTS 11
   Religious Inclusiveness and Sensitivity at the Funeral 11
   Special Religious Funeral Considerations .11
   General Information on Law Enforcement Funerals 13
   Elements of the Funeral 16
   Funeral Arrangements for Members Killed in the Line
       of Duty 20

SECTION III–LAW ENFORCEMENT FUNERALS

3. TYPES OF FUNERALS 29
   Funeral for a Member Killed in the Line of Duty 29
   Funeral for an Active Member Who Died Off-Duty 34
   Funeral for a Retired Member 34

SECTION IV–DEPARTMENTAL
ANIMAL MEMORIAL SERVICES

4. ANIMAL BURIALS 39
    A Rationale 39
    Memorial for a Departmental Animal Killed in the Line
        of Duty 39
    Memorial for the Death of Departmental Animal, Off-Duty
        or Retired 44

SECTION V–FUNERAL RESOURCES

5. READINGS AND SUPPORT 47
    Poems and Short Readings 47
    Police Hymns 52
    Prayers 53

SECTION VI–WHAT DO WE DO NOW?

6. SURVIVOR RESOURCES 61
    Survivor Resources, Helps and Supportive Agencies 61
    Support Agencies and Resources 66

SECTION VII–HOW DO WE PLAN FOR THE FUTURE?

7. LINE OF DUTY INJURY OR DEATH INFORMATION 71
    How do We Plan for the Future? 71
    The Funeral Supply Kit 76

Appendices:

A. *A Sample Line of Duty Death Departmental Regulation or*
    Standard Operating Procedure and Model Departmental Policy 79
B. *Funeral Checklist* 103
C. *Family Liaison Planning Team Checklist of Family Needs* 107
D. *For a Civilian Religious Officiant* 109
E. *Personnel Debriefings* 113

Endnotes 115

Index 119

ABBREVIATIONS

NRSV–the New Revised Standard Version translation of the Judeo-Christian Bible

RSV–the Revised Standard translation of the Judeo-Christian Bible

A PART OF AMERICA DIED

Somebody killed a policeman today
And a part of America died . . .
And a piece of our country he swore to protect
Will be buried with him at his side.

The beat that he walked was a battlefield, too,
Just as if he had gone off to war;
Though the flag of our nation won't fly at half-mast
To his name they will add a gold star.

The suspect who shot him will stand up in court
With counsel demanding his rights,
While a young, widowed mother must work for her kids
And spend many long, lonely nights.

Yes, somebody killed a policeman today . . .
Maybe in your town or mine,
While we slept in comfort behind our locked doors
A cop put his life on the line.

Now his ghost walks the beat on a dark city street,
And he stands at each new rookie's side;
He answered the call . . . of himself gave his all,
And a part of America died....

Harry Koch

(In memory of Patrolman John Burke, Atlantic City, New Jersey Police
Department, and all of the others killed in the line of duty.)

LAW ENFORCEMENT
FUNERAL MANUAL

Section I

WHERE DO WE START?

Chapter 1

PREPARING FOR THE FUNERAL

DEATH NOTIFICATIONS

Police chaplains and law enforcement personnel are usually called upon to make death notifications in the cases of death within their agencies and within the communities they serve. Notifying a person of the death of their loved one(s) is a task or role that requires careful preparation, sensitivity and planning. An excellent manual on recommended procedures for death notification has been published by the Iowa Organization for Victim Assistance (IOVA). This manual is entitled: *In Person, In Time.*[1] The following suggestions are offered to assist a department/agency with death notifications and death notification training.

1. Be prompt. Be timely. In-person notification should be made within two (2) hours of the event.

2. Make sure you have the correct information: the name of the person to be notified, the address where that person might be, the name of the person who died, how (if you can find out) that person died, and a telephone number where the person(s) being notified can find out more information about the death.

3. The notification is time-consuming. **Note: If the informing person doesn't have time to make the call (at least two (2) hours)–don't make the call! Get someone else to do it!**

4. Before arriving at the place where the notification is going to be made, decide who is going to give the notification. **One person should do the notification, supported by the other(s).**

5. Upon arrival, the one making the announcement identifies themselves and their official capacity. Such as: "I am Chaplain/ Officer _____." "I am with the _____ (agency)." Then introduce other members of the notification team.

6. Have the person(s) **sit down!** (They may faint or collapse and fall down upon notification.) Find out if there is anyone else in the home or business.

7. Then quickly, and as much to the point as possible, make the announcement in clear, plain language. A sample announcement might be: "I have some very difficult news to share with you. Your _____ has been killed." Always refer to the victim by their name, never by terms such as "body" or "corpse."

8. Next, wait for their reaction. **Whatever reaction they have is normal for them.** No two persons will react to tragic news in the same way. Expect the unexpected! In working with persons who are grieving, you need to be comfortable with it and allow it to happen. The chaplain/personnel should intervene only to prevent harm to them or others.

9. Your presence is what is important—a ministry of presence!

10. Give the person what is known, **but not why! Avoid euphemisms** (!) such as "God willed it . . . ." (He/She) was a brave (man/woman) . . . ." "You'll thank God for this some day," etc.

11. Listen, listen, listen! You will need to be comfortable with silence at this point.

12. Offer to make calls to other family members or have other chaplains make these announcements **in person.** If the immediate family lives out of town, arrange for another law enforcement agency to make a face-to-face announcement.

13. When leaving, **never leave the person alone!**–even if they ask for it. A support system must be in place prior to your departure: a faith leader, a member of their religious community, a family member, a friend, or a neighbor.

14. Leave a departmental/agency business card with the family in case they have any further concerns, questions or needs.

15. Reminder: The notification process cannot be rushed. If it is winter, take off coat(s) to indicate that you are going to stay for a while.

THE ROLE OF THE CHAPLAIN
IN DEPARTMENTAL FUNERALS

If the department/agency has a chaplain, the role of the Police Chaplain is to **ASSIST** the family, the family's faith leader (if any), and his/her fellow law enforcement officers through their sadness and grief. The chaplain can ask the family who will officiate at the service. If asked to conduct the funeral service, the chaplain's role is much broader than just the funeral itself. The ministry begins when the chaplain is first notified of the death of a law enforcement member and extends beyond the interment. The family needs immediate and continual support. (See pages 62–65 for specific information.) During the funeral, the chaplain comforts the bereaved and can pay tribute to the fallen officer. The chaplain serves as a counselor, spiritual advisor and friend to the family of the deceased.

Since the conduct of the funeral service honors the wishes of the family, the chaplain may be asked to cooperate with the family's faith leader if available. The funeral service is primarily spiritual and is properly a function of the local faith leader. The chaplain should accede to the desire of the civilian faith leader and the traditions of the religious organization/tradition of the family.

The police chaplain has a dual role: as a member of the law enforcement community and as a faith leader. The elements that the chaplain must balance are: the military style ceremony and the religious rite. The military style ceremony recognizes the service and sacrifice of a law enforcement officer; the religious rite extends a spiritual ministry of hope to the family, friends and the law enforcement community through worship.

Police chaplains are concerned with the totality of the grieving process. They should be quick to call upon the bereaved both before and after the funeral. It is important for chaplains to be available to the bereaved during the entire time of mourning. This mourning period may take a year or more. (See *Promoting Healthy Healing*, p. 62.)

If conducting the funeral service, the chaplain may be tempted to treat the elements of the service, other than the sermon or meditation, as secondary with the thought in mind that mourners are not really deeply affected by them. Yet other elements, i.e., prayer, scripture, poems, eulogies, these also speak of the reality of death, the answer of the faith and faithful, and the authenticity of grief. The chaplain's meditation is a matter of individual approach and style based on the mourning family's religious tradition. The funeral meditation brings the source of the mourner's faith tradition into contact with their needs. The chaplain should know the distinction between a meditation and the tribute or eulogy. Emphasis of the meditation should be pastoral rather than prophetic, comforting rather than chastising, edifying rather than evangelistic. Meditation texts should be short, appropriate, understandable, and memorable. The meditation should be judiciously brief, shared in the certainty of God's continued presence. Wisely used, the meditation can be an important aid in working through of the mourning process by those present.

The chaplain should wear the uniform or civilian clothes as authorized by her/his department or agency. An appropriate religious garment, the symbol of the office of the family's religious tradition, may be worn over the uniform of the chaplain.

During the funeral and burial services, opportunities will arise that will call upon the chaplain to use a military salute. The following is a guideline: if in uniform, a right-hand salute is rendered at the service; if in civilian clothing, the salute is rendered by placing the right hand over the heart.

Section II

ELEMENTS OF THE LAW ENFORCEMENT FUNERAL

Chapter 2

BASIC ELEMENTS

RELIGIOUS INCLUSIVENESS AND SENSITIVITY AT THE FUNERAL

Choosing the order of service and form is guided by the family's religion and/or denomination and the rituals and rules of that religion. Chaplains may officiate jointly with other faith leaders unless the laws and practices of the family's religion prohibit such co-officiation.

The police funeral must be more than simply a memorial ceremony. Special attention must be paid to the resources used in the service so that they meet the needs of the mourners. The service speaks of faith, joy, and assurance and does not necessarily center on a eulogy of the life or a display of the body of the deceased. The service provides the public confession of shared faith.

SPECIAL RELIGIOUS FUNERAL CONSIDERATIONS
(For Your Information)

Buddhist: In the course of Buddhism's movement throughout Asia it has taken on many forms and customs that are more reflective of the host culture where it was adopted than the original Indian tradition. As a result, it is difficult to identify specific protocols for assisting all Buddhist families. There are likely to be variations in the customs observed based upon the branch, denomination and/or cultural background of the officer's survivors.

For chaplains involved with Buddhist families the spirit of four pastoral "abilities" should be the basic consideration: availability, visibility, adaptability and credibility. Following these, the chaplain should approach the priest conducting the ceremonies or a family elder and inquire what the proper etiquette in supporting the family might be.

Hindu: Worship in the home is a paramount aspect of a Hindu funeral. The home of the deceased becomes the principal place of ritual. It is appropriate to personally bring flowers to the home of the deceased upon hearing of the death. In Hinduism, there is no concept of a "funeral home." The body of the deceased remains at the home of the family until taken to the place of cremation, which is usually within 24 hours after death. Flowers are placed at the feet of the deceased. The cremation ceremony is called *mukhagni* ("moo-KAHG-nee"). Casual dress for visitation and the cremation is appropriate. Head covering is not required. **White** clothing should be worn, **black** is **NOT** appropriate. Ten to fifteen days after the cremation, a mourning service is held at the family's home. This mourning is called the shraddha ("SHRAHD-hah").

Islamic (Muslim): [Definition: "islam" is the religion. The followers of Islam are called "Muslims."] Upon death, in Islamic tradition, the body is washed, placed in a shroud and buried before sundown. If this is not possible, burial takes place the next morning. Due to the length of time necessary for planning for a law enforcement officer's funeral, a memorial service should be considered. At the service no head covering is required for men. A dress is recommended for women that covers the arms and hems should reach below the knees. A scarf is required to cover the head for women. Dark and somber colors are advised. The wearing of religious jewelry or jewelry with faces or heads of animals or people is discouraged. The major officiant at the ceremony is called an "Imam." The Islamic holy scriptures are called The Qur'an. Muslims are never cremated. At the graveside the *Janazah* ("jah-NAH-zah") prayers for the dead are recited and the deceased is buried. Some examples of Islamic prayers are included in this manual (see page 55).

Jewish: Jewish funerals are customarily held as soon as possible after the death, but delays are acceptable under specific circumstances. A Rabbi must be consulted. Some examples of Jewish prayers are included in this manual (see pages 56–57). The use of flowers are usually discouraged at Jewish funerals.

Roman Catholic, Orthodox Catholic, Lutheran, Anglican:
Contact the local priest of the parish or the Ordinary for particulars on
the Rite of Christian Burial (the Funeral Mass).

GENERAL INFORMATION ON
LAW ENFORCEMENT FUNERALS

1. Family Liaison Planning Team
(See checklist, Appendix C, pages 107–108)

When law enforcement personnel die of any cause, the family of
the deceased must be consulted at every stage of the planning. A
Family Liaison Planning Team is strongly recommended and is usually assigned by the department/agency's head and/or his/her representative. This team is made up of a chaplain(s) and/or departmental
personnel (see pages 19–25). This team is assigned to assist the family
AND should in no way disrupt the plans or wishes of the family and
their faith leader and advisors. (See "For a Civilian Religious
Officiant" located in Appendix D, pages 109–111. This will assist this
person with their preparation and planning.) The planning team is to
carry out and facilitate the desires of the family. The team assigned
should be temporarily relieved of regular duties and placed on special
assignment for the duration of the funeral activities. This team needs
to be readily available to accommodate the planning activities associated with the funeral. The degree of involvement of those assigned to
assist the family is at the sole prerogative of the family. If a family faith
leader is going to conduct the funeral service, ask family if a Police
Chaplain or a Departmental Representative may speak on behalf of
the department/agency. If there is no family faith leader preference,
offer the services of the department/agency Chaplain. All plans, as
they develop, are communicated continually (as possible) to the chief
executive officer and other command personnel of the agency. The
chaplain(s) and/or personnel may also serve in an advisory role.

If the family does not wish to have a departmental funeral, their
wishes are to be honored. When a departmental funeral is not desired,
a departmental memorial service should be considered after the funeral. This memorial service, in circumstances when a departmental
funeral service does not occur, allows departmental personnel, area

law enforcement personnel, **AND** the community to pay their last respects to the deceased member. The family should be invited to that memorial service.

In some religious traditions, the funeral marks the beginning of a formal period of grieving that may last for a period of a month.

2. Hospital Visitation

Whenever possible, the departmental/agency chaplain/personnel should arrange for the family to visit their loved one as they cling to life (if conditions allow) and accompany the family to visit the deceased in the hospital. The law enforcement agency should provide transportation for the family, if departmental procedures allow. If departmental procedures do not allow for transportation, you will need to make these arrangements. This transportation should be to **and** from the hospital. The agency member transporting the family member(s) should wait patiently until they are ready to leave. Child care needs to be arranged for any children in the home. Food should be offered to the family as well as offering to have someone run errands for them.

3. Special Situations: Law Enforcement Suicide[2]

When assisting next-of-kin in suicide incidents, remove them from the immediate scene as quickly as possible and from the presence of the print and video media. Ask if the family has a faith leader that can be summoned. Again, if a family faith leader is going to conduct the funeral service, ask the family if a Police Chaplain or a Departmental Representative may speak on behalf of the department/agency. If there is no family faith leader preference, offer the services of the department/agency Chaplain. The following items are offered as helpful suggestions for suicide situations:

1. It is important that the department/agency makes the initial contact with the family.

2. Listen. Observe. Allow questions and conflicting remarks to surface.

3. Avoid being judgmental. Even when the survivors seek a judgment response, remain neutral and supportive.

4. Disregard .societal "taboos." Treat the bereaved with the same compassion and courtesy offered the victim of an accident or a fatal disease.

5. Help the family prepare a telephone response in case the print or video media does call. Suggest a family member be designated to answer the telephone and read a prepared statement, something similar to: "This is a representative of the family of (*name*). We appreciate your concern in our time of loss. We do not, however, have any further comment at this time. Thank you."

6. Offer to call other family members for them. For immediate family members who live out of the immediate area, request the law enforcement agency in that family member's area do the notification face-to-face.

7. Follow departmental procedures regarding transportation of next-of-kin, body identification, etc.

8. If the suicide occurred in a place where the family frequents, remove the family members from the scene as soon as possible. Immediately, after the scene is released from the departmental investigation, arrange for a cleaning of the scene before the family returns.

9. When ready to leave, offer condolences and leave a business card. The notification team will likely have begun to establish a rapport with the family and the card will be helpful if they have any concerns, questions or needs in the future. When leaving, **never leave the person alone!**–even is they ask for it. A support system must be in place prior to your departure: a pastor, a member of their congregation, a family member, a friend, or a neighbor.

10. The department should assign a member of the Family Liaison Planning Team to the family at this time to begin the planning process (see planning checklist on pages 107–108).

11. Immediately contact a suicide support group for the family and departmental personnel (see page 67).

Special Note: Some religious traditions have rules, customs, and rituals regarding suicide and suicidal burials. Competent religious authorities of those traditions must be consulted for guidance and information.

The suicide of a law enforcement member can deeply affect the family, law enforcement personnel AND the community. Questions, may arise, "How does taking one's own life endanger a person's soul?," or, "Does the act of suicide dishonor the badge?" Persons may also feel a deep sense of guilt for not being able to prevent the family member/departmental member from taking their own life. A suicide needs to be specifically addressed as a tragedy of circumstances that led their loved one, fellow departmental member and/or friend to feel that this was the only way out.

Remember, regardless of the cause of death, the deceased member was a "fellow officer" and that he/she will always be part of the "police family." The department or agency chaplain should continue pastoral contact. Departmental/Agency members are encouraged to do the same.

Ongoing training will need to be instituted for law enforcement members, particularly for their supervisors, on the clues and symptoms of suicide and what to do about such clues and symptoms if they are seen in their department's personnel. See "Support Agencies and Resources" section (pages 66–68) for immediate and ongoing help and support.

ELEMENTS OF THE FUNERAL

Most law enforcement funeral services are military in style. The following items are offered as a guide for those planning a law enforcement funeral service.

1. Pipe and Drum Corps

Pipers, or pipe and drum corps, have become a tradition at law enforcement funerals. If the department/agency does not have a pipe and drum corps, contacting a larger nearby city agency could be a source for such a corps for the funeral service. One piper may be sufficient in many circumstances.

2. Bugler

Military funeral services usually include a bugler or two to play taps at the conclusion of the graveside service. The second bugler is used as an echo to the first. Law enforcement services often follow this practice and utilize buglers. Again, if the department/agency does not have access to a bugler, contact a larger city agency to determine the availability for the service. The American Legion or The Veterans of Foreign Wars Post can also be a source of a bugler. An audiotape or compact disk recording of taps can also be used.

3. Honor Guard

Many departments/agencies have a special unit that serves special ceremonial functions for the department. The members of this unit may be issued special uniforms and/or equipment. There are a variety of functions that this unit can perform. For funerals, these functions might include: Color Guard, Casket Guard, Pallbearers and the Firing Detail.

1. The Color Guard carries and posts the National, State/Province, City and Departmental flags, if they exist, plus two guards (one on each side).

2. The Casket Guard consists of six to eight members and a member in charge. They stand guard in pairs, one at the head and one at the foot. The members of the guard should be changed every ten to fifteen minutes.

3. The Pallbearers (if requested) consists of at least six members to carry the casket and a member in charge. If a flag drapes the cas-

ket at the graveside, the Pallbearers will remove the flag from the casket, fold, and ready the flag for presentation to the family by the Department/Agency Head or his/her designee. (Practice folding the flag *before* the service!)

4. The Firing Detail consists of up to seven members and a member in charge. They fire a three-volley-gun salute during the service at the graveside. A 21-gun salute, seven members firing three volleys, is traditional. The members fire blank ammunition and can use shotguns, rifles or handguns for the salute.

4. United States Flag Etiquette[3]

The below listed United States flag etiquette is from the American Legion and the United States Flag Code. Other countries have similar traditions and regulations. Since most law enforcement funerals are military in nature, check with that country's armed forces for a source of specific flag etiquette.

Draping of the casket with a flag: The United States Flag Code states that although draping of the casket with an American flag is "usually reserved for veterans or highly regarded State and National figures, the Flag Code does not prohibit this use for an American citizen." Therefore, the American flag can be used to drape the casket of any United States fallen law enforcement member.

How to drape the casket: When the American flag is used to cover a casket, it should be so placed that the union [the blue field] is at the head and over the left shoulder of the deceased. The flag should not be lowered into the grave or allowed to touch the ground.

Folding the flag at the graveside: There is no United States Flag Code provision for folding of the flag. The traditional triangular military method for folding the American flag is described in Appendix A (pages 99–100).

Flying the flag at half-staff: The American flag, when flown at half-staff, should be first hoisted to the peak for an instant and then lower to the half-staff position. The flag should be again raised to the peak before it is lowered for the day. A State flag or any other flag or pennant in a display is lowered or removed when the Flag is at half-staff. No flag or pennant should be placed above the Flag of the United States.

Displaying the flag: When displayed from a staff in a religious institution or public auditorium, the flag of the United States of America should hold the position of superior prominence, in advance of the audience. If the flag is on the platform with the speaker, the flag is placed to the right of the speaker. If the flag is on the level with the audience, the flag is placed to the right of the audience. (For more information check the website: usflag.org) Any other flags so displayed should be placed on the left of the clergy person or speaker or to the right of the audience.

Displaying a flag across a street or at an entrance to a cemetery: When the flag is displayed across and over the middle of a street, it should be suspended vertically with the union to the north in an east and west street or to the east in a north and south street. Flags are often displayed over the middle of a street as a way of marking the funeral procession route to the cemetery or at the entrance to the cemetery.

5. Badge Mourning Bands

Black or royal blue badge mourning bands are usually worn at law enforcement funerals. They are 3/8 to 1/2 inch wide bands placed horizontally across the center of the badge. These bands can be purchased at most police supply houses. (In an emergency, black electricians' tape can be used as a substitute.)

6. Flowers

White carnations, tinged with red, could be used as a boutonniere for those attending. The stems of the carnations can be slipped under the attending officers' badges, facing downward. The boutonniere, pinned upside down, could also be pinned to the clothing of those not in uniform or where the carnation will not fit or stay under the badge. As a sign of final respect, at the grave site and at the conclusion of the service, the carnations can be removed and placed on the casket as those in attendance pass by the casket in front of the family and immediate friends.

[**Note:** *The use of flowers at Jewish funerals is discouraged.*]

7. Ribbons

Blue ribbons, 1/4 inch wide and looped like a cursive "L," could be pinned to the uniforms and clothing of those attending the funeral service. Metal gold and blue looped ribbon pins may be purchased from the funeral home or a religious supply store. The metal pins can be more solemn and are more enduring than fabric ribbons.

FUNERAL ARRANGEMENTS FOR MEMBERS KILLED IN THE LINE OF DUTY[4]
[For a Funeral Checklist, see Appendix B, pages 103–105.]

Since there will be a large gathering of law enforcement and related personnel, consideration should be given to advise the local division of Homeland Security of the plans.

Funeral Arrangements

Phase I

1. Immediately assign a Family Liaison Planning Team, consisting of a police chaplains(s) and/or departmental personnel, to the family members of the deceased member recognizing the religious tradition (if any) of the family. (See pages 107–108 for Family Liaison Planning Checklist.) If the family has a faith leader, invite that person into the planning process as quickly as possible. (Offer the faith leader a copy of "For a Civilian Religious Officiant," see pages 109–111.)

2. The assigned police chaplain(s) or law enforcement officer(s) remains available and do whatever is needed to assist the family in any way until after the funeral.

3. If the family desires, arrange for official notification of other immediate family members of the officer. If these family members live out of the area, consideration should be given to asking another law enforcement agency to notify the family member

face-to-face. (**Note:** A police chaplain of a particular faith may not fulfill the needs of a deceased member. This consideration is especially important when the member and his/her family are from another religion. A list of clergy from all identifiable religions might be compiled and kept available. Religious representatives are generally supportive when requested by the police agency to aid families of their particular faith.)

4. The chaplain(s) or personnel involved with the arrangements will work with the family to meet all of their wishes for the fallen member's funeral. They will share with the family of the member by informing them of what is available to them and work closely, sensitively and carefully with them in the planning process of the funeral service. The chaplain(s)/departmental personnel will work directly with the funeral home director. Funeral home directors appreciate this assistance to effect a smooth transition.

5. Guard the family from the print or video media. Help the family prepare a telephone response when the media does call. Suggest a family member be designated to answer the telephone and read a prepared statement, something similar to: "This is a representative of the family of (*name*). We appreciate your concern in our time of loss. We do not, however, have any further comment at this time. Thank you."

6. It has been suggested that a police legal advisor, or legal representative of the governmental entity, should be assigned to the planning team. Having an attorney available from the outset may seem premature; consider however, the situation when there is a family dispute over who has the right to make the arrangements (particularly when the deceased member has been divorced, has grown children, etc.). An attorney can prove indispensable in such awkward situations, and "buffer" police officials from becoming embroiled in these dilemmas. Legal assistance can also be useful in determining the proper release of the deceased member's personal belongings and other potential predicaments.

Phase II

After the initial shock and preliminary plans have been made for the law enforcement member's funeral, the following are to be done:

1. The print and video media. While it is important that the print and video media be informed on the basic facts surrounding the death of the member, it is crucial that the family members of the deceased are shielded from the media.

2. A remembrance bulletin or card should be compiled. The information in the bulletin could include a photograph of the fallen member, their family history, work history, possibly even something off the member's original application of why they wanted to be a law enforcement officer. Suggested poems and readings for inclusion can be found in Chapter 5 (pages 47–51). This bulletin should be readied and sent to the printer during the first day after the member's death so it can be ready for the service.

3. If the family desires it, arrange for music during the funeral service. The funeral director can assist in obtaining a person to play and/or singing for the service if held in a secular setting. If a religious institution is being used, the institution can assist with obtaining a person(s). Pre-recorded music can be used for the service. A compact disk has been recorded for law enforcement funerals and memorials by Catherine Mortiere. The CD is entitled *I don't know how to say goodbye.* A copy of the CD can be obtained by contacting the International Conference of Police Chaplains at (850) 654-9736, FAX (850) 654-9742, or icpc@gnt. net.

4. During the funeral service, list all law enforcement agencies that are in attendance so that the chief departmental officer can send a thank you note to those departments that attended to pay their tribute to the deceased member.

5. If a visitation or wake is a part of the family's religious tradition, a casket guard should be included in the planning. The casket guard is normally made up of six to eight (6 to 8) representatives

of the member's department (if the fallen member's department is small, seek representatives from surrounding departments and/or agencies). These members of the casket guard would stand two at a time, one at the head and one at the foot of the casket, at a 45-degree angle to that casket. They stand at attention while visitors view the deceased. These members should be in full dress uniform with headgear and white gloves. The casket guard remains until the family has left the facility. Change the casket guard every ten to fifteen minutes. The members of the casket guard that are relieving those stationed at the casket, will come to attention in front of the casket, salute the casket and then in a military fashion, change places with the officers that have been standing guard. The relieved members of the guard then face the casket, salute the casket, do an about-face, and march away.

6. The casket guard, in pairs: one at the head and one at the foot, may stand at the casket during the beginning portion of the funeral service. Once the service begins, they sit down and return at the conclusion of the funeral service, prior to the dismissal of the congregation. When the casket is removed from the funeral home, religious institution, or building, the casket guard, along with all uniformed personnel from the fallen member's department or agency, will make two parallel lines from the doors of the facility to the hearse. All other department/agency personnel will stand in ranks behind these two lines. The casket guard will also be present at the grave site.
   Note: This portion of the service will need to be carefully planned. Every formation will be different depending upon the physical layout of the facility being exited and the adjacent parking facilities.

7. The pallbearers, chosen in consultation with the family, consist of at least six (6) persons and one (1) person in charge. They are present at the funeral home and, if used, the religious institution. At the cemetery, if a flag is used to drape the casket, the pallbearers are responsible for folding the flag for presentation to the family (see pages 99–100 for folding an American flag). (Practice folding the flag *before* the service!)

8. As the casket approaches, the casket guard comes to attention and salutes until the casket and the family members have passed by. The same procedure is done at the cemetery from the hearse to the grave site. After the grave site service is over and immediately after the benediction, everyone is called to attention and "Taps" are played.

9. The entire family should be chauffeur-driven by uniformed personnel of the member's department/agency, or by funeral home personnel, to the visitation, the funeral and the grave side services where appropriate. They should be taken home after the meal or time of refreshment. The order of the vehicles in procession from the funeral home, or the funeral facility, to the cemetery are as follows: (1) the deceased member's department vehicles not involved as lead vehicles, (2) the other agency's vehicles, (3) the lead police vehicles, (4) the funeral director and chaplain/religious officiate, (5) the police vehicles for pallbearers, (6) the hearse, (7) a flower vehicle (if used), and (8) the member's family and friends.

10. All police and emergency vehicles travel in the procession with their emergency lights, head lights and flashers on. A tow truck should be available in case of a vehicle breakdown. Two law enforcement members should remain at the home of the deceased during the entire time required for the funeral rites. It is appropriate, if possible, for the funeral procession to go by the member's departmental headquarters or command post on the way to the cemetery. It would also be appropriate to have the route pass by the deceased member's home. To pay a final tribute, at either the home of the fallen member or at his/her headquarters, a contingent of uniformed personnel could be there, if so, they are called to attention and salute, as the hearse and family drive by. Civic facilities and schools should also be considered to be driven by when planning the route.

11. Many departments come a long distance. Housing arrangements should be arranged for these department members at nearby hotels or motels. The host department/agency should provide a light meal for these officers if a meal is not provided after the

funeral. This meal will give the personnel an opportunity to visit with other law enforcement members and share their feelings and concerns with one another.

12. Resource persons are very much needed during the time of a law enforcement member's death and funeral service. They may be asked to do such things as baby sit, provide transportation, clean house, prepare meals, wash dishes, be part of a support system, etc. These persons need to be those who want to be there because they care. They very often might be able to minister to the deceased member's family better than anyone else.

13. It should be the deceased's law enforcement department's/ agency's responsibility to supply a person(s) to assist the family during any court proceedings as a consequence of the deceased member's death. This assisting person(s) would support the family during the trial if they choose to attend the trial. This person(s) also would remain with them and keep away print and video media and people whose intentions are not worthwhile.

14. Badge mourning bands or black arm bands, at a minimum, are worn by members of the deceased member's agency from the time the member died until midnight of the day the member is buried. Mourning bands are worn at law enforcement funeral services by all uniformed personnel. Generally, these mourning devices are only worn beyond the funeral services when a member is killed in the line of duty. The length of time that the member's agency wears these devices will depend upon the agency's/department's policies.

15. Bunting over the doors of the department is very appropriate. The bunting material is black and is placed over the main entrances to the police facility. The bunting can remain for thirty days after the death of the member. At a minimum the time the flag flies at half-mast at the member's department is until midnight of the day the member is buried. The length of time may be extended based upon the agency's/department's policies.

16. It is important to provide security during the time of a law

enforcement member's funeral arrangements and at the deceased member's home. This is to observe people and watch police vehicles and property belonging to officers from other departments. This needs to be done in a very organized and systematic manner.

17. It is also important that the department watch our for "helpful" attorneys who may have a desire to negatively help the family. Attorneys sometimes contact deceased member's families for lawsuits of many different kinds. The chaplain(s) or personnel should make the family aware of this and that they should not discuss any matters with anyone other than an attorney that they know and trust.

18. Memorial Contributions: It is not uncommon, as a result of the death of a police member, that individuals and civic groups may wish to donate money and/or other contributions in the name of the member or for his/her family. The police agency should have a policy governing memorial contributions to avoid indecision and inconsistency. Moreover, public relations will be enhanced because inquirers can be appraised how monies will be accepted and possibly even provide a list of memorial options available.

19. Funeral services without immediate graveside committal: Some graveside committal services will be delayed because of circumstances surrounding the time or location of burial. In these circumstances, the procession to the cemetery will not take place and the service would terminate at the conclusion of the funeral service itself. A police honor guard or contingent of the departmental/agency members should accompany the deceased until burial occurs.

20. Out-of-state/region Burials: When burial of the deceased member occurs in another region and requires transportation of the body, a suitable escort should be arranged to accompany the body. In consultation with the slain member's family, arrangements should also be made with the law enforcement agency/agencies of that region for an appropriate graveside committal service.

Section III

LAW ENFORCEMENT FUNERALS

Chapter 3

TYPES OF FUNERALS

FUNERAL FOR A MEMBER KILLED IN THE LINE OF DUTY

A Suggested Service

Instrumental Prelude

Opening Sentence (suggestion)

The Lord is my light and my salvation; whom shall I fear? The Lord is the stronghold of my life; of whom shall I be afraid? . . . . Though an army encamp against me, my heart will not fear; though wars arise against me, yet I will be confident. One thing have I asked of the Lord, whom will I seek after, to live in the house of the Lord all the days of my life, to behold the beauty of the Lord, and to inquire in His temple. For the Lord will hide me in His shelter in the day of trouble; the Lord will conceal me under the cover of His tent, He will set me high upon a rock. . . . I believe that I will see the goodness of the Lord in the land of the living. Wait for the Lord; be strong, and let your heart take courage; wait for the Lord! (Psalm 27:1, 3–6; 13–14, NRSV)

Invocation Prayer (suggestion)[5]

O God, what a Friend You have been. When we have been lonely, You have encouraged us. When serving, You have supported us. When struggling, You have strengthened us. Now in our deep distress, as we pass under the shadow of great affliction, lonely in bereavement –O God, Intimate Friend, comfort us with Your presence at this moment. Fill our desolate hearts with peace and with pride, so that we may cling closely to You, who is able to turn shadows of night into morning light. Amen.

Readings, Poems (see pages 47–51, for suggestions)

Scripture Readings (some suggestions)
    Psalm 23; 36:5–7; 46:1–3, 10–11; 56:1–6, 8–11; 90; 103 or 130 (or any others)

Eulogy (if desired)

Pastoral Prayer (two suggestions—or see pages 53–57)
    Eternal God, Lord of Life, to whom the ranks of life report, we bow before You with reverent hearts and in sublime faith, knowing that You lead us on in death as You do in life. For again You have ordered a comrade to that realm beyond the twilight and the evening star, where beauty and valor and goodness dwell forever with the unnumbered multitude. Mindful of service nobly done, You have called (*name*) to everlasting rest. You have sealed (*his/her*) lips. With the faded blossoms of springtime and the withered leaves of autumn, You have called (*him/her*) to Eternal Peace, to the land of Your silent mystery.
    We know only that You, O God are Life and Light and Love. You smile in the shaft of gleaming sunlight and in the tender light of stars. You mourn with us in the drizzling rain and settling dew. Hear now the sorrows of those who mourn. Touch their tired hearts with healing. Protect them with Your holy care. Keep clean and bright in memory the splendid flame that now has flickered out, and shelter us with Your compassion.
    Accept the pledges of our hearts and increase the purpose of our souls. Draw for us from the departed, increased devotion to the best and noblest things of life. Join us with (*name*) in communion with the goodly fellowship of those who fell in the cause of justice; with all who have died to defend the rights of people and the good faith of our communities and nation; with those who have strove mightily that righteousness might prevail and liberty endure; and finally with those whose daily lives are an offering to duty and their (*political entity and country/nation*). Inspire us by these examples of integrity and bravery. Amen.[6]

or

Holy God, in these moments of remembrance, lift our hearts and minds above the shadowy darkness of death to the light of Your presence. We thank You for the life of our comrade now removed from our association. We are grateful for (*name's*) devotion to a law enforcement officer's duty, for (*his/her*) dedication to the preservation of life and property, for the way (*he/she*) faced danger in (*his/her*) service to the community.

We ask the comfort of Your blessing upon (*name's*) family. May they be sustained by pleasant memories, a living hope, the compassion of family and friends, and the pride of duty well done. Grant them peace and freedom from fear. Finally, we pray your guidance and strength for those who continue to battle the foe. Keep all who devote themselves to the work of law enforcement safe. Amen.[7]

Hymn (if desired) (see pages 52–53 for suggestions)

Meditation Example[8]

We have gathered here to honor (*name*) who lived life to the fullest, every atom aglow. It is most fitting that we have come here to convey sympathy and love to the family and loved ones in the death of this brave (*Deputy/Officer/Trooper*). In a true sense, it is a mutual loss to the family and to this community (*or political entity*) for whose protection (*he/she*) laid down (*his/her*) life.

It is utterly appropriate that we express corporately the gratitude we feel for this (*Deputy's/Officer's/Trooper's*) service, and the sterling dimensions of spirit and helpfulness (*name*) always demonstrated. All the more difficult it is to accept (*his/her*) untimely death.

When death strikes suddenly and senselessly, by some tragic, bewildering process, our minds question *Why?* A multitude of questions involving the motive and ways of God, and the future estate of your loved ones surface in your thoughts. The death of (*Deputy/Officer/Trooper*) (*name*) has raised many difficult problems for this family and (*department/agency*) to resolve. It is a fruitless inquiry. We can never prove in a scientific laboratory, the nature of God, or the soul, or the substance of the spiritual. Many of life's most profound realities we assimilate into life before achieving scientific proof. Clearly we do not know the whole story. However, the promise is that one day we will know and understand, even as God now understands.

Our religious faith teaches us that we live our present life in a world that is not our true home. As a household of faith, we come to convey love to this grieving family and (*department/agency*). We come to share your loss, and to pray for God's guidance and support.

If we can keep perspective, we will be comforted. It is God who heals the brokenhearted, by bidding us to recall the blessed days of fellowship and companionship. Do not put the days of joy and happiness out of your conversations and thoughts. Indeed, we have come here to recall the good gift God has given us in sharing the life and character of (*name*).

[*Review some of the enduring characteristics of the departed*]

Closing Poem or Short Reading (a suggestion—or see pages 47–51)

"Miss Me"
(author unknown)

Miss me . . . but let me go.
When I come to the end of the road, and the sun has set for me.
    I want no rites in a gloom-filled room.
Why cry for a soul set free?

Miss me . . . a little, but not too long.
And not with your head bowed low. Remember the love that
    we once shared.
Miss me . . . but let me go.

For this is a journey that we all must take, and each must go
    alone.
It's all a part of the Master's Plan. A step on the road to home.

When you are lonely and sick at heart, go to the friends we
    know and bury your sorrow in doing good deeds.
Miss me . . . but let me go.

Benediction (suggestion)
O God, grant us the vision of the Invisible, that in the face of death,

we will see You face-to-face, and rejoice in Your presence, anticipate the reunion with loved ones and friends, and find courage and peace forevermore. In Your holy name. Amen.

Postlude

Procession to the Cemetery

The motorcade route to the cemetery should be as direct as possible. The route could include the fallen officer's police facility, *his/her* home, the community's civic center and schools.

The following is a suggested order of vehicles in the motorcade:

❑ 1. The first police vehicles will be those from the department of the fallen officer.
❑ 2. All other police and emergency vehicles not directly involved in the funeral service.
❑ 3. The lead police vehicles from the member's department/agency (these may be motorcycles).
❑ 4. The funeral director and police chaplain/religious officiant.
❑ 5. The police vehicles for pallbearers.
❑ 6. The hearse.
❑ 7. A flower carrying vehicle, if used (this could be a fire truck).
❑ 8. The member's family and friend's vehicles.

Note: It is advisable to have a tow truck available in case of a vehicle breakdown.

Upon arrival at the cemetery. The police and emergency vehicles, all lights turned off, are parked and the uniformed law enforcement personnel are assembled. [**Note:** Consideration should be given to allowing spouses of law enforcement personnel to stand by their spouse in this formation at the cemetery.] When the hearse arrives at the cemetery, a pipe and drum corps can be added to lead procession of the hearse to the grave site. If a color guard is to be used, they would follow the pipe and drum corps. Next, if desired, a saddled, riderless horse with boots placed in the stirrups backwards, can also be added to lead the procession. The flower vehicle, if used, would be dropped off at this point and the flowers taken to the grave site. The immediate family vehicle(s) would follow the hearse. Honorary pallbearers can be added to walk beside the hearse to the grave site. At the grave site the vehicle or vehicles are unloaded and parked. The pallbearers go to the hearse and carry casket to the grave site.

FUNERAL FOR AN ACTIVE MEMBER WHO DIED OFF-DUTY

A funeral service for an active member who dies while off-duty, not in the line of duty, is often difficult to conduct because of the feeling for that member. While full respect needs to be accorded to the member, they were not killed or died in the performance of their law enforcement function. The funeral service is conducted within the guidelines that the agency/department has established. The preceding funeral arrangements and the service can be utilized or adapted for such a service.

FUNERAL FOR A RETIRED MEMBER

The funeral for a retired member of a law enforcement agency deserves special attention. The years of dedicated service that the member gave to his/her department or agency and their community are commendable. A funeral service can be drawn from the preceding funeral service and supporting material provided in this manual. Upon learning of the death, the department/agency should consider assigning a police chaplain, or designated representative to the family to assist their preparations. If practical, personnel from the retired member's department and a marked police vehicle should be sent to the funeral service. An honor guard should also be considered. The chaplain can assist the family's faith leader or, if requested, conduct the service. The chaplain and any official representative(s) of the deceased member's department/agency should be in full dress uniform.

The following two poems could be included in a funeral service or graveside committal:

1. **Prayer for a Retired Member**[9]

(She/He) walked life's lonely path with honor, Lord,
    Protecting those you sent (her/his) way . . .
Until, at last, with task well done,
    Your call is heard today.

I hear You saying:
"Come, my friend, with me . . . from years of service rest.
    You've helped the poor, protected all, you've passed life's every
    test.
You did not falter, did not fail though weary was your soul.
    I saw your tears, I felt your fears . . . I helped you toward your
    goals."

"Beneath that badge there beat a heart strong, courageous, true . . .
    When duty called, you answered, a hero dressed in blue!

Come, my friend, your reward awaits. The law you did obey.
    Faithful through life's endless storms you showed my people
    the way."

"Your beat is ended; roll call is done! Now, rest on Heaven's shore.
    The good you did so willingly will be remembered forever
    more."

Thank you; Father, for your great love as we cherished (her/his)
memory dear.
    We offer this brave soul to you . . . be with (her/him) ever near.
And when, at last, we hear your call may we each take our place.
    On Heaven's shore, eternal home, beneath your kindly gaze.

and/or

2. **Come! Rest!**[10]

Now, come and rest at last, my friend, your duty's ended; your job
well done.
    The years you spent in others' need your God's final reward
    has won.

I saw the dreams you set aside to serve my people in danger, poor.
  Nobility took you far beyond mere "job" as loneliness, fatigue
  you endured.
You dared to go where others feared—with courage, life's beat you
trod . . .
  Knowing well that when you served, you did the work of God.
You laid down the badge but not the love that marked with honor
all your days . . .
  I watched, affirmed, blessed, refreshed your spirit along life's
  ways.

Come! Rest, my friend, your duty's o'er. Drum beat and Taps
proclaim,
  Stand tall with ranks of heroes blue! Hear God pronounce your
  name . . .

Be blest, my noble friend! Come, rest!

Section IV

DEPARTMENTAL ANIMAL
MEMORIAL SERVICES

Chapter 4

ANIMAL BURIALS

A RATIONALE

Most animals are not given a formal memorial service. The following items, in this section, are offered to assist a department/agency in creating a formal or informal service for a deceased departmental animal. An animal serving a law enforcement agency whether killed in the line of duty, died off-duty or died of natural causes in retirement, deserves a memorial service for the dedication that animal and his/her trainer(s) and/or handler(s) gave to the department/agency. The department/agency's personnel and the community the animal served often need a memorial service to honor this animal because of their memories and remembrances of the animal–this is particularly true for school children who may have met the animal and formed an attachment.

MEMORIAL FOR A DEPARTMENTAL ANIMAL KILLED IN THE LINE OF DUTY

A Suggested Service

Instrumental Prelude (suggestion): "All Things Bright and Beautiful"

Opening Sentences (suggestion): Then God said to Noah and to his family with him. "As for me, I am establishing my covenant with you and your descendants after you, and with every living creature that is

39

with you, the birds, the domestic animals, and every animal of the earth with you, as many as came out of the ark." (Genesis 9:8–10, NRSV)

A Thought (suggestion): "All things bright and beautiful, all creatures great and small, all things wise and wonderful: The Lord God made them all" [the refrain from the above hymn, "All Things Brights and Beautiful"]. The animals of God's creation share in the fortunes of human existence and have an essential part of human life.

Invocation Prayer (suggestion)[11]

Creator God, to those who never had a (*dog or horse*) as a partner, this prayer will sound strange, but to you, God of all life and Creator of all creatures, it will be understandable.

Our hearts are heavy as we face the loss in death of our beloved (*animals' name*) who was so much a part of the life of (*Deputy/Officer/Trooper*) (*name*).

This (*Canine/Equine*) partner made life more enjoyable and gave cause to laugh and to find joy and security in (*animal's name*)'s company. We remember and give thanks for the fidelity and loyalty of this partner. We will miss (*him/her*) being with us.

From (*animal's name*) we learned many lessons, such as the quality of naturalness and the unembarrassed request for affection. In caring for (*his/her*) daily needs, we were taken up and out of our own self-needs and thus learned again the service of others.

Creator God, may the death of this creature of Yours remind us that death comes to all of us, animal and human, and that it is the natural passage for all life. May (*animal's name*) sleep on in eternal slumber in Your godly care as all creation awaits the fullness of Your final liberation. Amen.

Scripture Reading (a suggestion):
Psalm 121

Reading or Poem (six suggestions):

1. **General:** A Reading from a Blessing of Animals[12]
   The animals of God's creation inhabit the skies, the earth and the sea. They share in the fortunes of human existence and have a part

in human life. God, who confers His gifts on all living things, has often used the service of animals or made them symbolic reminders of the gifts of salvation. Animals were saved from the flood and afterwards made a part of the covenant with Noah (Genesis 9:9–10). The paschal lamb brings to mind the Passover sacrifice and the deliverance from the bondage of Egypt (Exodus 12:3–14); a giant fish saved Jonah (Jonah 2:1–11); ravens brought bread to Elijah (1 Kings 17:6); animals were included in the repentance enjoined on humans (Jonah 3:7).

2. **General:** A Reflection on the life of Saint Francis of Assisi[13]
   Francis saw the tiny worm lying in his path, and he stopped to pick it up, because it was a creature of the Almighty. He saw the wild flowers of the fields, but even more he saw the hand of God that made them. . . . But always he saw, more than anything else, that all things were intended to touch the hearts of men [*and women*] and lift them to God.

3. **K-9:** "Tribute to a Dog"[14]
   The one unselfish friend that anyone can have in this selfish world, the one that never will desert them, the one that never proves ungrateful or treacherous, is their dog. A dog will stand by you in prosperity and poverty, in health and sickness. [*He/She*] will sleep on the cold ground where the wintry winds blow and the snow drives fiercely, if only [*he/she*] may be near [*his/her*] master's side. [*He/She*] will kiss the hand that has no food to offer, [*he/she*] will lick the wounds and sores that come with an encounter with the roughness of the world. [*He/She*] guards the sleep of [*his/her*] pauper master as if they were a prince or a princess. When all other friends desert, a dog remains. When riches take wings and reputation falls to pieces, [*he/she*] is as constant in [*his/her*] love as the sun in its journey through the heavens.

4. **K-9:** "The First and Last Police Canine"[15]
   The first to sense the hostility of a suspect.
   The first to react to protect his master.
   The first to enter where danger lurks.
   The first to detect the hidden intruder.
   The first to take action against violence.

The first to sense [*his/her*] master's joy.
The first to know [*his/her*] master's sorrow or fear.
The first to give [*his/her*] life in defense of the person who is
    [*his/her*] master.
The last to be forgotten by those who work with others like
    [*him/her*]. They know [*him/her*] as a partner, not just an animal.

5. **K-9:** "Your Police Canine"[16]
[*His/Her*] eyes are your eyes
    To watch and protect you.
[*His/Her*] ears are your ears
    For your safeguard in the dark.
[*His/Her*] nose is your nose
    To scent, track and lead you.
[*His/Her*] life, with no greater love
    Is yours, so you may live.

6. **General:** "He Refreshes the Soul of His Master"[17]
        (author unknown)
Commitment, loyalty, faithfulness, these are qualities that set a person apart from the crowd. They are qualities that we expect to find in the line of those who chose to serve in areas of responsibility. But in the life of (*handler's or trainer's*) (*name*) these qualities are given of (*his/her*) own free will.

But how do you measure, or how do you explain these qualities in the behavior of an animal that cannot understand them as qualities that are recognized as above the normal reaction?

To them loyalty, faithfulness, obedience, is the only response they know or can give. That is why it is important that we have this ceremony in recognition of those unique qualities that in fact led to (*animal's name*)'s death.

As Proverbs 25:13 suggests of (*animal's name*) behavior, (*he/she*) was a "faithful messenger to those who sent [*him/her*] refreshes the spirit of (*his/her*) masters" (RSV). May we take notice in the days and weeks ahead to make every effort to at least do as much . . .

Pastoral Prayer

Hymn (optional)

Scripture (suggestion): Genesis 1:1, 20–25

Suggested Meditation Example[18]

Commitment, loyalty, faithfulness . . . these are qualities that set a person apart from the crowd. We expect to find these qualities in the life of those who choose to serve in areas of responsibility. But in the life of a Peace Officer these qualities are given of (*his/her*) own free will.

How do you measure, or how do you explain these qualities in the behavior of an animal that cannot understand them as qualities that are recognized as the normal reaction? To them loyalty, faithfulness, obedience is the only response they know or can give. That is why it is important that we have this ceremony in acknowledgment of those unique qualities that in fact led to (*animal's name*)'s death. That (*equine/K-9*) partner, who is unable to be with us today because of a prior and distinct commitment.

So today, in this service, we thank God for giving us (*animal's name*). We thank God too for the training (*he/she*) received and the handling (*Deputy's/Officer's/Trooper's*) (*name*) gave (*him/her*). We thank God for (*Deputy's/Officer's/Trooper's*) (*name*) and for the other handlers and (dogs/horses) that assist in keeping the citizens of our community (or political entity) safe and our department personnel alert and aware. We acknowledge (*Deputy's/Officer's/Trooper's*) (*name*) and (*animal's name*) value and the value of (*K-9 Units/Mounted Patrols or* _____) and programs throughout our jurisdictions, state, and nation. And above all we extend condolences to (*title: Deputy/Officer/Trooper plus full name and rank*) at the loss of (*his/her*) very special partner. May our gracious God patch that hole in your soul . . . may God be pleased to do that through those of us gathered here.

And let me add this, (*Deputy's/Officer's/Trooper's*) (*name*), men and women of law enforcement and fellow citizens . . . quite often, as a Chaplain, I'm asked if "animals go to heaven?" I have my own prejudices and thoughts on this subject. Part of the answer can be drawn from the Bible for in Genesis 1:24–25 we read: "And God said: 'Let the earth bring forth living creatures of every kind . . .' And it was so. . . . And God saw that it was good" (RSV). That's a commentary on such as (*animal's name*).

(*Deputy's/Officer's/Trooper's*) (*name*) that's good enough for me and I pray that it is a comfort for you!

Benediction

Postlude

At the Burial Site

Deputies/Officers/Troopers could form a double line through which the animal, or the animal's cremains, are carried to the place of interment. In respect to the animal's memory and service, all departmental members formally participating in the memorial service should be in full dress uniform. A blank rifle, shotgun, or pistol volley and taps could be used to conclude the service.

MEMORIAL FOR THE DEATH OF DEPARTMENTAL ANIMAL, OFF-DUTY OR RETIRED

A Suggested Service

A memorial service could be gleaned from the preceding section and the following suggested prayer:

A Suggested Prayer for a Dog that Died of Old Age[19]
You've given many gifts, oh Lord, that brighten, help and cheer, like butterflies and sunset skies.

But of the gifts there's none more dear than a dog who shares our smiles and cares with a friendly wagging tail, or a look with ever caring eyes into our own, as though they were studying each thought we have.

And when their short, good lives are done and they have gone away, they leave a sorrow.

Yes, but too, a joy that still does stay on through the years ahead, and brings a tear but most a smile, for what they shared with you and I helped make our lives worthwhile.

Section V

FUNERAL RESOURCES

Chapter 5

READINGS AND SUPPORT

POEMS AND SHORT READINGS

1. "Ode to a Fallen Comrade"[20]

There are some who look for glamour in the uniform of blue;
   Seeing only high adventure, but, oh, if they only knew –
For the law enforcement officer (his/her) duty's never done.
   (His/Her) battle's never over and (his/her) war is never won.
(He/She) must face with courage new perils of each day.
(He/She) must rise above the scornful, they don't understand or
   care that to guard the rights of others is the reason that
   (he's/she's) there.
You, our dear and fallen comrade, have personified the best, gave
   your all in the line of duty, with sheer bravery, and passed the
   test.
In our hearts, now touched with sadness, you'll be with us to the
   end.
   For our lives will be better having had you for a friend.

2. Law Enforcement Memorial Prayer at Graveside or Chapel Ceremonies[21]

Dear Lord, Law Enforcement is not an easy task to do.
   Yet there are many who choose to wear the shield.
They serve each day, to the oaths they swore are true,
   Protecting and serving, a safer, better world to build.

Lord, now we gather to pay our deepest honor,
    To one of ours, an officer, killed in the line of duty.
It matters not the style of the shield they wore,
    Only that they served with pride and honorably.

Lord all that matters is that they were one of us,
    Serving wherever needed, from rich mansion to dirtiest alleys
Confident and proud, highly honored by the peoples trust,
    So they carried a shield, mindful of all their sacred duties.

Lord you have called one of us home to glory,
    The race with life for this one is now done.
Peace, blessed peace in safety forever now with Thee,
    Welcome rest, now in heaven for all of eternity.

May times never erase the sacrifice that was made,
    May no officers ever fall alone, to lie cold in their grave.
May those of us still serving remember well the price they paid,
    May their memory stand forever as one who went down brave.

Lord give us the courage to carry on, to still live and care,
    To not be vengeful or bitter, to simply trust your word is true.
May we always cover with pride the shield we wear,
    To honor all fallen officers whom we now commend to you.

3. **"Part of America Died"**[22]
(In memory of Patrolman John Burke, Atlantic City Police Department, New Jersey–and all of the others killed in the line of duty)

Somebody killed a policeman today and part of America died . . .
And a piece of our country [*he/she*] swore to protect
Will be buried with [*him/her*] at [*his/her*] side.

The beat that [*he/she*] walked was a battlefield, too.
Just as if [*he/she*] had gone off to war;
Though the flag of our nation won't fly at half-mast
To [*his/her*] name they will add a gold star.

The suspect who shot [*him/her*] will stand up in court
With counsel demanding his rights
While a young, widowed mother must work for her kids (*or appropriate surviving family statement*) and spend many long, lonely nights.

Yes, somebody killed a policeman today . . .
Maybe in your town or mine,
While we slept in comfort behind our locked doors
A cop put [*his/her*] life on the line.
Now [*his/her*] ghost walks the beat on a dark city street,
And [*he/she*] stands at each new rookie's side;
[*He/She*] answered the call . . . of [*himself/herself*] gave [*his/her*] all.
And a part of America died . . .

4. "Policeman's 23rd Psalm"[23]

The Lord is my Shepherd, I shall not want.
    His comforting hand reduces fear to naught;
He makes me walk through streets of crime,
    But He gives me courage and peace of mind.

He leads me by still waters in the path I trod,
    And He says in Romans I'm a "minister of God;"
He leads in righteousness as He restores my soul.
    For His name's sake He keeps me whole.

When I walk through death's valley, right up to the door,
    I will fear no evil, for He comforts me more;
For Thou art with me every step of the way,
    As thy rod and thy staff protect me each day.

He prepares a table, especially for me,
    As I work daily among life's enemies;
His gives me authority to uphold the law,
    And He anoints my position in the midst of it all.

Surely goodness and mercy shall follow me,
    Each day of my life through eternity;

As I long to hear Him say, "Well done . . . ,"
When I lay down my life, my badge, and my gun.

5. "When God Made Peace Officers"
(anonymous)
(read at Indiana State Trooper Jason Beal's Funeral Service,
January 20, 2000)

When the Lord was creating Peace Officers, He was into His sixth
day of overtime when an angel appeared and said "You're
doing a lot of fiddling around on this one."

And the Lord said, "Have you read the specs on this order? A
peace officer has to run five miles through alleys in the dark,
scale walls, enter homes the health inspector wouldn't touch,
and not wrinkle [*his/her*] uniform."

"[*He/She*] has to be able to sit in an undercover car all day on a
stakeout, cover a homicide scene that nights, canvass the neigh-
borhood for witnesses, and testify in court the next day."

[*He/She*] has to remain in top physical condition at all times, run-
ning on coffee and half-eaten meals. And [*he/she*] has to have six
pair of hands."

The angel shook her head slowly and said "Six pair of hands . . .
no way."

"It's not the hands that are causing the problems," said the Lord.
"It's the three pair of eyes an officer has to have."

"That's on the standard model?" asked the angel.

The Lord nodded. "One pair that sees through the bulge in a pock-
et before [*he/she*] asks, 'May I see what's in there, sir?' when
[*he/she*] knows already [*he/she*] should have taken that account-
ing job."

"Another pair here in the side of [*his/her*] head for [*his/her*] partner's safety. And another pair of eyes in the front that can look reassuringly at a bleeding victim and say, 'You'll be all right, ma'am.' When [*he/she*] knows it isn't so."

"Lord," said the angel, "rest and work on this tomorrow."

"I can't," said the Lord, "I already have a model that can talk a 200 pound drunk into a patrol car without incident, and feed a family of four on a civil paycheck."

The angel circled the model of the peace officer very slowly. "can it think?" she asked.

"You bet," said the Lord. "It can tell you all the elements of a crime, recite the Miranda warnings in its sleep, detain, investigate, search and arrest a gang member on the street in less time than it takes five learned judges to debate the legality of the stop and still keep its sense of humor. This officer also has phenomenal personal control. [*He/She*] can deal with crime scenes painted in hell, coax a confession from a child abuser, comfort a murder victim's family, and then read in the daily paper how law enforcement isn't sensitive to the rights of criminal suspects."

Finally the angel bent over and ran her finger across the cheek of the peace officer. "There's leak," she pronounced. "I told you that you were trying to put too much into this model."

"That's no leak," said he Lord. "It's a tear."

"What's the tear for?" asked the angel.

The Lord said, "It's for bottled up emotions, for fallen comrades, for commitment to that funny piece of cloth called the American flag, for justice."

"You're a genius," said the angel.

The Lord looked somber, "I didn't put it there," He said.

POLICE HYMNS

1. "Amazing Grace, The Policeman's Tribute"[24]
(sung to the tune: "Amazing Grace")
[suggested instrument: bagpipes]

    1. (verse one from the original hymn)

    2. A man in blue has lost his life in service of the law. The love that makes the sacrifice is the greatest love of all.

    3. A police–man was killed today, the reason why I can–not say. I don't know why he had to die. The man in blue died for me and you; we must re–mem–ber him too.

    4. Flags fly low, let us bow in prayer for fal–len pol–ice–men every–where; and re–mem–ber this: that they are missed. The badge bright like an eve–ning star free from a world of war.

    5. (verse five from the original hymn)

    5. (alt.) The sor–row that be–reaves us now, a sor–row of the world, our Lord will great–er kind–ness show, a–bove make spir–its whole.

2. "Police Hymn"[25]
(Sung to the tune: "MELITA")

    1. O Lord of sir–ens and scout cars, of pre–cincts, crui–sers, stripes and stars, of off–i–cers whose lives are cast a–mong the hero–es un–sur–passed; Give us the courage, strength, and skill to nobly act, our roles ful–fill.

    2. O Thou in whom we find our peace, en–gage our hearts as po–lice we may not yield to bit–ter–ness as when ex–posed to dai–ly stress. From vi–o–lence and hu–man greed, Lord, save us, so that we may lead.

    3. E–ter–nal Fa–ther, in whose hands, we place our lives at Thy

com–mand, Whose voice of strength will calm our fears, "Be not a–fraid, for I am near," O Lord of Peace, be with us now. In Thee we trust will be our vow. A–MEN.

3. "Come Home"[26]
(sung to the tune: "How Great Thou Art")

1. A new day dawns, the voice of God now thunders
   like trumpet blast from that eternal shore.
   "Arise, my friend, you wore your badge with honor,
   receive instead this crown forevermore."

Refrain:
   Your shift is fin–ished and earth's duty done;
   Life's battle o'er, the victory won.
   The time of tears and burdens now all cease
   Come forth, my friend, stand tall in peace.

2. I saw the pain, the anguish of your service,
   the gift of life for others you laid down.
   I walked with you when darkness seemed around you
   and truth so noble in your heart I found.

Refrain:
   Your shift is fin–ished and earth's duty done;
   Life's battle's o'er, the victory won.
   The time of tears and burdens now all cease . . .
   COME HOME, my friend. Stand tall in peace!

PRAYERS

1. A Prayer[27]

Lord of my aching heart: (*He/She*) was so young, so very young, with all of life before (*him/her*). Exuberant, vital, full of promise, of breathless wonder. Gifted, intelligent, sensitive, always inquisitive, eager to learn, to know, to do . . .
Admired by (*his/her*) friends, loved, so dearly loved.

Lord, no longer dare I beat my fists upon the walls of Heaven. I am too weary, too sorrow-consumed. I know now that ten thousand whys will never bring (*him/her*) back.

In pitch darkness I have shouted my whys. My reward? A sea of shadowed silence. What is left? What more shall I ask?

Just this dear God: Think through me Your thoughts. Create within me Your peace until there is born in my aching heart "The trust of the unexplained."

2. St. Augustine: A Prayer of Comfort[28]

God of our life, there are days when the burdens we carry chafe our shoulders and weigh us down; when the road seems dreary and endless, the skies gray and threatening; when our lives have no music in them and our hearts are lonely, and our souls have lost their courage.

Flood the path with light, we beseech Thee. Turn our eyes to where the skies are full of promise. Tune our hearts to brave music.

Give us the sense of comradeship with heroes and saints of every age and so quicken our spirits that we may be able to encourage the souls of all who journey with us on the road of life.

To Thy honor and glory.

3. A Prayer for Hope and Joy in Times of Sorrow[29]

Eternal God, who has been the hope and joy of many generations, and in all ages has given men and women the power to seek You and in seeking to find You: grant us, we pray, a clearer vision of Your truth, a greater faith in Your power, and a more confident assurance of Your love.

If we cannot find You, let us search our hearts and know whether it is not rather we that are the ones that are blind rather than You who are obscure, and we who are fleeing from You rather than You from me.

4. A Prayer for Strength[30]

Be Lord,
    within me to strengthen me,

without me to preserve,
over me to shelter,
beneath me to support,
before me to direct,
behind me to bring back,
round about me to fortify.

Islamic Prayers

1. A Prayer from Mohammed[31]

We are born asleep and at death we awake.

2. A Prayer for Strength[32]

Lord of men, who givest life and bringest to death, thou art the beginning and the end, the First and the Last, unchanging in every scene.

Keep us this and every day, in the path of life. Grant us strength according to our time. Unite our days in one. Let thy compassion go before and follow after us, that in the detail of our lives we may find the proof of thy mercy. For unto thee is our becoming and our returning. Amen.

He gives life and he makes to die and to him you shall be returned.

3. The Fatiha (the opening of the Qur'an)[33]

In the name of God, the Compassionate, the Merciful
Praise be to God, Lord of the Creation,
The Compassionate, the Merciful,
King of Judgement-day!
You alone we worship, and to You alone we pray for help.

Guide us to the straight path
The path of those whom You have favored,
Not of those who have incurred Your wrath,
Nor of those who have gone astray.

Jewish Prayers

1. Jewish Prayer for Mourners[34]

O Lord,
Who healest the broken-hearted
And bindest up their wounds,
Grant thy consolation unto the mourners . . .

O strengthen and support them
In the day of their grief and sorrow;
And remember them (and their children)
For a long and good life.

Put into their hearts the fear and love of thee,
That they may serve thee with a perfect heart;
And let their latter end be peace. Amen.

2. Jewish Memorial Prayer[35]
(Recited at the funeral, memorial service or at graveside)

O Lord and King,
Who art full of compassion,
God of the spirits of all flesh,
In whose hand are the souls of the living and the dead,

Receive, we beseech thee,
In thy great Loving kindness
The soul of (*name of deceased*)
Who hath been gathered unto (*his/her*) people

Have mercy upon (*him/her*)
Pardon all (*his/her*) transgressions,
For there is none righteous upon the earth,
Who doeth only good, and sinneth not.

Remember unto (*him/her*)
The righteousness which (*he/she*) wrought,
And let (*his/her*) reward be with (*him/her*).

And (*his/her*) recompense before (*him/her*).

O shelter (*his/her*) soul in the shadow of thy wings.
Make known to (*him/her*) the path of life:
In thy presence is fullness of joy;
At thy right hand, bliss for evermore.

3. **Jewish prayer for the sanctification of God's name, the Kaddish**[36]
(This prayer is offered at the graveside)
[**Note.** The Kaddish prayer is traditionally recited in the presence of ten adult male Jews.]

Mourner's Kaddish:
Magnified and sanctified be the great name of God throughout the
world which He hath created according to His will.
May He establish His kingdom during the days of your life and
during the life of all the house of Israel, speedily, yea, soon; and
say ye, Amen.

Congregation and Mourners:
May His great name be blessed for ever and ever.

Mourners:
Exalted and honored be the name of the Holy One, blessed be He,
whose glory transcends, yea, is beyond all blessings and
hymns, praises and consolations which are uttered in the
world; and say ye, Amen.

May there be abundant peace from heaven, and life for us and for
all Israel; and say ye, Amen.

May He who establisheth peace in our heavens, grant peace unto
us and unto all Israel, Amen.

Section VI

WHAT DO WE DO NOW?

Chapter 6

SURVIVOR RESOURCES

SURVIVOR RESOURCES, HELPS
AND SUPPORTIVE AGENCIES

"Taking Care of Our Own"[37]

A United States Department of Justice, National Institute of Justice "Research In Brief" document (1997), states that a staggering sixty-seven percent (67%) of law enforcement agencies surveyed lacked formal policies concerning the death of a member.

The same document revealed that departments are also lacking guidelines for continued emotional support for the survivors beyond the days of the visitation and funeral.

Failure to provide continued support for the surviving family gives them the impression that they have been "totally handicapped" by the department/agency. A survivor's level of distress is affected by the department's response to the tragedy of the line of duty death.

A common myth is that a surviving family will "get over" the tragedy and will simply move on with their lives; that a grieving individual will simply allow the tragedy to become part of their personal history and put it behind them.

What the department/agency and co-workers do not understand is that the family and loved ones suffer and grieve each time an anniversary occurs, whether it is an anniversary of a positive event (i.e., wedding, baptism, birth of a child) or a negative event (i.e., anniversary of the deceased member's death, father/mother's day, the deceased's birthday, etc.).

Another myth within the law enforcement community is that the type of death a member encounters, felonious or accidental, somehow affects or impacts the grief and pain suffered by the surviving family. Studies reveal that whether a member dies accidentally, off-duty, or feloniously on-duty, does not impact a family any greater than the other. Accidental death and/or off-duty deaths are no less heroic a death than felonious, on-duty deaths. All deaths are devastating to the loved ones left behind, regardless of the circumstances. A department/agency or co-worker's response to the nature or details of the member's death greatly affects the grieving and bereavement period of the family. Please note that the actions and behaviors of the law enforcement family, and even agencies in the surrounding community, impacts the grieving of the survivors. Departments/Agencies and law enforcement personnel must be careful and aware of the attitude and words that are being spoken to the loved ones of a member who has died. Hidden nuances and body language that indicate that the member somehow was at fault or "simply screwed up" can add several years of additional grief and unanswered questions to the survivors' pain and suffering.

"Promoting Healthy Healing"[38]–A Helpful Checklist

1. Healthy healing begins immediately at the time of death with a face-to-face notification. This message needs to be delivered in person, in time, in pairs, in plain language and with compassion.

2. An essential part of promoting healing is to immediately assign a planning team to answer the telephone, ensure food is available, make telephone calls as necessary, run errands and do anything within reason the family requires. This could include discussing with the family if they would like to open a trust fund for young children(s) for donations (discuss the placing of a child's name on the account because of probate reasons).

3. Additionally the planning team will: Confer with the family in regard to their wishes, inform the family of facts of law enforcement funerals so they can make knowledgeable and well-informed decisions (realize that the family's final choices are "law," and are not to be overruled to accommodate opinions of

the department/agency) and escort the family on both days of the visitation and the funeral.

4. It is important that the Public Safety Officer's benefits and insurance policies be reviewed and discussed at a home meeting held within five (5) days of the funeral, discuss survivors benefits, and then again another meeting should take place again at thirty (30) days in the same detail. The department needs to file all necessary papers, including performing all the paperwork for the family in a timely manner, keeping the family abreast of the status of the paperwork on a regular basis. These meetings should also include what benefits are available to the survivors through state Worker's Compensation laws and what is provided through federal agencies and information on departmental/agency insurance, medical coverage for surviving families, college tuition for children, etc.

5. Honoring the fallen hero:
    Some departments/agencies provide a twenty-four (24) hour "watch" or Honor Guard with the deceased from the time of death until the burial (this is for the surviving family and their comfort).

6. Following the visitation and funeral: Daily visits should be made by individuals within the department/agency to the family to see if they require anything, and to validate they are not being "abandoned." These visits should continue for several weeks following the funeral, they do not have to be lengthy, just a contact to see how the family is doing and to show concern on behalf of the department/agency. Over the course of the first six (6) months, a family should be visited or taken to lunch at least once every one to two weeks. Continued contact should remain for a least one (1) full year. Cards should be sent randomly throughout the year from different shifts within the department, or from different departmental members. The department/ agency should be sure to invite the family to all luncheons, dinners, retirement parties— anything to keep them in contact with the department/agency (this validates that they continue to remain in the brotherhood/ sisterhood and in the law enforcement family). The department should make available to the family all press and media coverage, stories, departmental/agency photographs, etc.

7. Memorials and ceremonies in honor of the deceased member: The department should escort the spouse, children and parents to any ceremony in which the officer is being honored. Any expenses incurred by the family when attending a memorial ceremony in honor of the fallen member should be considered for reimbursement (this would/could include ceremonies offered locally, within the state, or in Washington, D.C. during National Police Week).

8. Do not assume that the family has been contacted by another organization, such as the State Lodge of the Fraternal Order of Police or other agency, that a ceremony is being held to honor the fallen member. It is the department's responsibility to contact the survivors and inform them of the honor to be bestowed upon their loved one at the ceremony. A departmental vehicle should be provided. Flowers should also be brought for the family, corsages for the women. [**Note:** For a Jewish family, check with a Rabbi to see if flowers are appropriate for such services.]

9. **Important!** The **first** year of death is just a rehearsal, the **second** year of the loss, is actually living with the loss.

10. Healthy healing is continued when special occasions/holidays/ birthdays are remembered: Send birthday cards to each of the children and spouse on their birthdays (a small gift of some type is not amiss); send a card on the deceased member's birthday letting the family know that the department is aware of their loss on this special day; send flowers and a card on the wedding anniversary; make sure to send a Christmas card (if appropriate) and, if no family lives in the area, invite the family to another member's home for a holiday dinner (Thanksgiving, Christmas Eve and Christmas (if appropriate) or other religious holidays). Consider serenading the family in the driveway by playing Christmas carols over the PA system and with lights flashing; place a call on New Year's Eve to soften the coming of another year without their lived one; buy Christmas gifts (if appropriate) for all the children, spouse and parents; hold occasions for coffee or luncheons at the department to continue to make the surviving family feel they "can stop by" and are still part of the law enforcement family;

provide the family with departmental paraphernalia, such as watches, badge necklaces; continue to send a copy of the departmental newsletter (if produced) to the surviving family members; attend the graduations of the children and buy a graduation gift; place a street or highway sign in memory of the fallen hero at the one-year anniversary of their death; dedicate a tree at the department in memory of the fallen hero at the one-year anniversary (tied with a blue ribbon of honor).

11. Grave site visitation and honors: Visit the grave site on anniversaries and special occasions (like: the anniversary of the member's death), leaving a flower or flag to let the family know that someone from the department cared and remembered. [**Note:** For a Jewish grave visitation, a stone left on the marker is the appropriate ways to honor the dead.]

12. Preserve memories for the surviving family by creating a video of the different officers from within the same department and other departments, that worked closely with the deceased officer, telling stories. Have the funeral videotaped with all the law enforcement personnel paying their respects and honor and offer to the family around six (6) months to a year after the death. Almost every family wants a copy when offered later, however most will not think of it at the time of the death. This is especially true if children under the age of five are present. If the family declines, file the video away for possible contact by a child after they reach adulthood.

13. Discover the hobbies of the spouse, children and parents of the deceased member: take or participate in the events and/or hobbies that interest the survivors (i.e., if the spouse likes to golf, take him or her golfing, if they like to garden, take them flowers to plant, if the children like to play softball, go watch a game, etc.).

Please note: All of the above items are intended to stimulate a department or agency to create their own way of promoting healthy healing within their organization for the surviving spouse, children and family of their fallen law enforcement member.

SUPPORT AGENCIES AND RESOURCES

Support Agencies/Persons

COPS (Concerns of Police Survivors, Inc.), P.O. Box 3199, South Highway 5, Camdenton, MO 65020, telephone: (573) 346-4911; FAX (573) 346-1414;
COPS Webpage: *http://www.nationalcops.org*
COPS E-Mail: *cops@nationalcops.org*
(COPS provides continuing support for survivors. Their motto is: "Reaching out to help America's police survivors." COPS offers a book, "Better not Bitter; The Story of Concerns of Police Survivors" by Connie Clark. This is the story of COPS and a copy can be obtained from the above address. COPS offers a quarterly newsletter *COPS Newsletter.* They also have information on Federal benefits available to survivors.) (Check and see if your state has a local branch of COPS.)

International Conference of Police Chaplains: office address: P.O. Box 5590, Destin, Florida 32540; office telephones: (850) 654-9736, FAX (850) 654-9742;
E-mail: icpc@gnt.net, Web-site: www.icpc4cops.org.

Laurie A. Erickson, Inc., Independent training consultant, P.O. Box 415, Howell, Michigan 48844-0415, (810) 634-7634, FAX (810) 227-1689, E-Mail: *tblofmi@ismi.net* (Thin Blue Line of Michigan, a support organization for families after a line of duty death).

The National Law Enforcement Officers Memorial Fund, 400 7th Street NW, Suite 300, Washington, DC 20004, Web Site: www.nleomf.com (the fund will accept gifts in the name of a fallen officer), (202) 737-3400.

Bereavement Resources

American Association of Retired Persons (AARP) Widowed Persons Service, 601 E Street, NW, Washington, DC 20049, (800) 687-2277,
http://www. aarp. org/griefandloss/organization.html

American Association of Suicidology, 5221 Wisconsin Avenue, NW, Washington, D.C. 20015, (800) 273-8255, FAX (202) 237-2282, *http.//www.suicidology.org.*

Personnel Debriefing

CISD/CISM: The International Critical Incident Stress Foundation, Inc., 3290 Pine Orchard Lane, Suite 106, Ellicott City, Maryland 21042, (410) 313-2473, FAX (410) 750-9601, *http://www.icisf. org.*

NOVA: National Organization for Victim Assistance, 510 King Street, Suite 424, Alexandria, Virginia 22314, (703) 535-6682, *http://www.try-nova.org.*

Law Enforcement Suicide

American Association of Suicidology, 5221 Wisconsin Avenue, NW, Washington, D.C. 20015, (800) 273-8255, FAX (202) 237-2282, *http://www.suicidology.org.*

The National P.O.L.I.C.E. Suicide Foundation: contact Executive Director Robert E. Douglas, Jr., 8424 Park Road, Pasadena, Maryland 21122, (866) 276-4615, *http://www.psf.org.* The foundation offers a police suicide bulletin entitled: "No way out . . . **WRONG!** There is a way."

Victim Assistance Resources

Laurie A. Erickson, Inc., Independent training consultant, P.O. Box 415, Howell, Michigan 48844-0415, (810) 634-7634, FAX (810) 227-1689, E-Mail: *tblofmi@ismi.net* (Thin Blue Line of Michigan, a support organization for families after a line of duty death).

Mothers Against Drunk Drivers (MADD), 511 East John Carpenter Freeway, Suite 700, Irvine, Texas, (800) 438-6233, FAX (972-869-2206, 24-Hour Helpline (877) 623-3435, *http://www.madd.org*

NOVA: National Organization for Victim Assistance, 510 King Street, Suite 424, Alexandria, Virginia 22314, (703) 535-6682, *http://www.try-nova org.*

Office for Victims of Crime (OVC), U.S. Department of Justice, 810 7th Street, NW, Washington, D.C. 20531, (202) 616-3574, *http://www.ojp.usdoj.gov/ovc.*

Public Safety Officers Benefits Program, U.S. Department of Justice (provides Federal death benefit of $283,385–as of October 1, 2005), (888) 744-6513.

Section VII

HOW DO WE
PLAN FOR THE FUTURE?

Chapter 7

LINE OF DUTY INJURY OR
DEATH INFORMATION

HOW DO WE PLAN FOR THE FUTURE?

This section provides you with the basic information that you should have prior to the unexpected death of one of your departmental or agency members.

A form, "Line of Duty Injury or Death Information," is included in this manual. It is from the Mt. Vernon Police Department, Mt. Vernon, Illinois. This form is offered as an example of what you might develop for your department or agency. While this form is essential and important, it must be updated on an ongoing basis, at least annually. If this form is not updated it is useless since your member's family statuses are always changing as well as their contact information.

The contents for a Funeral Supply Kit are suggested.

CONFIDENTIAL

Line of Duty Injury or Death Information

****

Name _____

                Last   First   Middle

The information that you provide on this form will be used ONLY in the event of your serious injury or death in the line of duty. Please take the time to fill it out accurately because the data will be of extreme comfort to your family and the Mt. Vernon Police Department.

Line of Duty Injury or Death Information Form Continued

Your Address _____

City _____

State _____ Zip Code _____

Your home phone number (_____) _____

FAMILY INFORMATION

Spouse's Name _____

Address and Telephone _____
(if different from above)
_____
_____

Spouse's employer _____
work address and
telephone number _____
_____

Names and dates _____ DOB: _____
of birth of your
children who live _____ DOB: _____
with you.
_____ DOB: _____

_____ DOB: _____

_____ DOB: _____

If you are divorced, please provide information about your ex-spouse.

Name _____

Address _____

Line of Duty Injury or Death Information Form Continued

City   _____

State   _____ Zip Code _____

Home Phone   (_____) _____

Work Phone   (_____) _____

Do you want a police representative to contact your ex-spouse?

           ( ) yes   ( ) no

Please list the name, address, and telephone numbers of your children who live outside the family home and key relatives (parents, siblings, in-laws, etc.) below:

Name	Address	Phone (Home & Work)	Relationship
1.			
2.			
3.			
4.			
5.			
6.			

MEDICAL INFORMATION

Physician's Name   _____

Blood Type   _____

Existing Medical Conditions and/or Allergies   _____

_____

_____

_____

Line of Duty Injury or Death Information Form Continued

NOTIFICATION

Who would you designate to contact your family in case of line of duty injury or death?

_____

Is there anyone you would like to accompany the person you specified when the notification is made to your immediate family? If someone other than a Mt. Vernon Police Department Officer, please include address and telephone number.

1. _____

2. _____

Please list the persons you would like to be contacted in case of serious injury or death in the line of duty. Begin with the first person you would like notified.

Name	Address	Phone (Home & Work)	Relationship
1.			
2.			

Is there anyone you would like contacted to assist your family, or to assist with funeral arrangements and/or related matters who is not listed above? This person should be knowledgeable concerning your life insurance representatives, location of your will, etc.

Name	Address	Phone (Home & Work)	Relationship
1.			
2.			

ADDITIONAL INFORMATION

Please list any preferences you may have regarding funeral arrangements:

Funeral Home _____

Church or Synagogue _____

Cemetery _____

Line of Duty Injury or Death Information Form Continued

Are you a veteran of the U.S. Armed Services?   (   ) yes   (   ) no

If you are entitled to a military funeral as
determined by the Department of Veterans
Affairs, do you wish to have one?   (   ) yes   (   ) no

Do you wish a law enforcement funeral?   (   ) yes   (   ) no

Please list memberships in law enforcement, religious, or community organizations
that may provide assistance to your family.

_____   _____

_____   _____

_____   _____

Do you have a will?   (   ) yes   (   ) no

If yes, where is it located?   _____

Please list any insurance policies you may have.

	Company	Policy #	Location of Policy
1.			
2.			
3.			

Are there any special requests or directions you would like followed upon your
death?

_____

_____

_____

_____

_____

Line of Duty Injury or Death Information Form Continued

_____

_____

_____

_____

_____

Signature _____ Date _____

THE FUNERAL SUPPLY KIT

It is strongly suggested that a funeral supply kit be created and maintained/refilled by each department or agency. The following items should be considered in this kit:

- Black (or blue) mourning ribbons, enough for all department/ agency members
- A dozen pairs of white gloves in various sizes
- Blank ammunition for the firing detail
- List of needed functions and roles for the funeral:
  Family Liaison Planning Team members and contact information
  Honor Guard members and contact information
  Color Guard members and contact information
  Pipe or Pipe and Drum Corps contact information
  Bugle player contact information or prerecorded tape
  Local state Concerns of Police Survivors contact information
- A copy of this funeral manual

APPENDICES

Appendix A

A SAMPLE LINE-OF-DUTY DEATH DEPARTMENT REGULATION OR STANDARD OPERATING PROCEDURE AND MODEL DEPARTMENTAL POLICY

The city of Buchanan is a small city located in Berrien County, Michigan, in the lower southwestern corner of the state. Buchanan has a population of 4,500 persons and covers approximately four square miles.

The Police Department consists of the following:

One (1)	Chief of Police
Two (2)	Sergeants
Six (6)	Full-time Police Officers
Five (5)	Part-time Police Officers
Fourteen (14)	Reserve Police Officers

The Department also has:

Four (4)	Volunteer Police Chaplains

And, an active Boy Scout Explorer Post.

Buchanan Police Department: Officers, Reserves, Chaplains and Explorers (1999)

Note: From Buchanan Police Department, city of Buchanan, Michigan.

Buchanan City Police Department
Line-of-Duty Death or Serious Injury
General Order 19
Revision Date: 05-01-99

I. PURPOSE

The purpose of this order is to establish procedures that will ensure the proper support and emotional care for a Buchanan City police officer's family following a line-of-duty death.

II. POLICY

It is the policy of the Buchanan City Police Department to provide liaison assistance to the family of any member who dies in the line-of-duty. This assistance will be provided whether the death was unlawful, suicidal, accidental (automobile accident, hit by a passing vehicle during a traffic stop, training accident, etc.), while the officer was performing a police-related function (either on- or off-duty), and while the officer was an active member of the Department. Members include full-time and part-time officers, reserve officers, civilian personnel, chaplains, and former/retired members of this Department. The Chief of Police may institute certain parts of this order at his/her discretion for special circumstances surrounding any member's death (active or former member). The Department will also provide a clarification and comprehensive study of any survivor benefits as well as other tangible and intangible emotional support during this traumatic period of readjustment for the surviving family. Funeral arrangements of the deceased member are to be decided by the immediate survivors with their wishes taking precedence over the Department's. The Department will provide assistance with the arrangements if requested by the family. The Department chaplain shall determine if he/she may be of assistance to the Chief of Police helping the family of the deceased in any way.

III. ASSISTANCE FOR AFFECTED OFFICERS

A. Officers who were on the scene or who arrived moments after an officer was critically injured or killed should be relieved as quickly as possible.

B. Police witnesses and other officers who may have been emotionally affected by the serious injury or death of another officer will attend a Critical Incident Stress Debriefing.

IV. DISCUSSION

Coordination of events following the line-of-duty death of a police officer is an extremely important and complex responsibility. Professionalism and compassion must be exhibited at all times as an obligation to the officer's family and to the law enforcement community. In order to provide the best possible services and support for the officer's family, specific tasks may be assigned to selected members of the Department. Their titles are:

A. NOTIFICATION OFFICER

B. HOSPITAL LIAISON OFFICER

C. FAMILY LIAISON OFFICER

D. DEPARTMENT LIAISON OFFICER

E. DEPARTMENT CHAPLAIN

F. BENEFITS COORDINATOR

An explanation of each of these responsibilities is contained in this order. An officer may be called upon to perform more than one role.

V. PROCEDURES AND RESPONSIBILITIES

A. NOTIFICATION OFFICER

1. It shall be the responsibility of the shift supervisor to properly notify the next of kin of an officer who has suffered severe injuries or died. The shift supervisor may personally make the

notification, designate a NOTIFICATION OFFICER to inform the survivors, or contact a(n) Department chaplain(s) to respond to the location(s).

2. The name of the deceased officer *MUST NEVER* be released by the Department before the immediate family is notified.

3. If there is knowledge of a medical problem with an immediate survivor, medical personnel should be available at the residence to coincide with the death notification.

4. Notification *MUST ALWAYS* be made in person and never alone. The Chief of Police or a representative, police chaplain, close friend, or another police survivor could appropriately accompany the NOTIFICATION OFFICER. However, if the aforementioned persons are not readily accessible, notification should not be delayed until these people can gather. If there is an opportunity to get to the hospital prior to the demise of the officer, *DON'T* wait for the delegation to gather. The family should learn of the death from the Department FIRST and not from the press or other sources.

5. NEVER make a death notification on the doorstep. Ask to be admitted to the house. Inform family members slowly and clearly of the information that you have. If specifics of the incident are known, the NOTIFICATION OFFICER should relay as much information as possible to the family. Be sure to use the officer's name during the notification.

   If the officer has died, relay that information. Never give the family a false sense of hope. Use words such as "died" and "dead" rather than "gone away" or "passed away."

6. If the family requests to visit the hospital, they should be transported by police vehicle. It is highly recommended that the family NOT drive themselves to the hospital. If the family insists on driving, an officer should accompany them in the family car.

7. If young children are at home the NOTIFICATION OFFICER must arrange for babysitting needs. This may involve coworkers' spouses, transportation of children to a relative's home, or a similar arrangement.

8. Prior to departing for the hospital, the NOTIFICATION OFFICER SHOULD notify the hospital staff and the HOSPITAL LIAISON OFFICER (by telephone if possible) that a member(s) of the family is enroute.

9. The deceased or severely injured officer's parents should also be afforded the courtesy of a personal notification if possible.

10. If immediate survivors live a significant distance beyond this Department's jurisdiction, the NOTIFICATION OFFICER will ensure that the Communications Division sends a teletype message to the appropriate jurisdiction requesting a PERSONAL notification. The NOTIFICATION OFFICER may choose to call the other jurisdiction by telephone in addition to the teletype message. Arrangements should be made to permit simultaneous telephone contact between the survivors and the Department.

11. The Chief should respond to the residence or the hospital to meet with the family as quickly as possible.

12. In the event of an on-duty death, the external monitoring of police frequencies may be extensive. Communications regarding notifications should be restricted to the telephone whenever possible. If the media has somehow obtained the officer's name, they should be advised to withhold the information pending notification of next of kin.

B. HOSPITAL LIAISON OFFICER

1. The Chief of Police will assign an officer to be the HOSPITAL LIAISON OFFICER. The HOSPITAL LIAISON OFFICER is responsible for coordinating the activities of the hospital personnel, the officer's family, police officers, the press, and others. These responsibilities include:

    a. Arrange with hospital personnel to provide an appropriate waiting facility for the family, Chief of Police, the NOTIFICATION OFFICER, and only those others requested by the immediate survivors.

    b. Arrange a separate area for fellow police officers and friends to assemble.

c. Establish a press staging area.

d. Ensure that medical personnel relay pertinent information regarding an officer's condition to the family on a timely basis and before such information is released to others.

e. Notify the appropriate hospital personnel that all medical bills relating to the injured or deceased officer be directed to the municipality, workers compensation insurance carrier, or the Department. The family should not receive any of these bills at their residence. This may require the HOSPI-TAL LIAISON OFFICER to re-contact the hospital during normal business hours to ensure that proper billing takes place.

f. Ensure that the family is updated regarding the incident and the officer's condition upon their arrival to the hospital.

g. Arrange transportation for the family back to their residence.

2. If it is possible for the family to visit the injured officer before death, they should be afforded that opportunity. A police official should "prepare" the family for what they might see in the emergency room and should accompany the family into the room for the visit if the family requests it. Medical personnel should advise the family of visitation policies and (in the event of death) explain why an autopsy is necessary.

3. The NOTIFICATION OFFICER(S) should remain at the hospital while the family is present.

4. Do not be overly protective of the family. This includes the sharing of specific information on how the officer met his demise, as well as allowing the family time with the deceased officer.

C. FAMILY LIAISON OFFICER

1. The Chief of Police (or a designee) will meet with the officer's family at their home to determine their wishes regarding Departmental participation in the preparation of the funeral or services. All possible assistance will be rendered.

2. With the approval of the family, the Chief will assign a FAMI-LY LIAISON OFFICER. The Chief will also designate a DEPARTMENT LIAISON OFFICER and a BENEFITS COORDINATOR.

   The selection of FAMILY LIAISON OFFICER is a critical assignment. An attempt should be made to assign someone who enjoyed a close relationship with the officer and his family.

3. This is not a decision-making position. This is a role "facilitator" between the family and the Department.

4. Responsibilities of the FAMILY LIAISON OFFICER:

   a. Ensure that the *needs of the family* come before the wishes of the Department.

   b. Apprise the family of information concerning the death and the continuing investigation.

   c. Provide as much assistance as possible, including overseeing travel and lodging arrangements for out-of-town family members, arranging for food for the family, meeting child care and transportation needs, etc.

   d. Be constantly available to the family.

   e. Determine what public safety, church, RAM/Love (Red Bud Area Ministries), fraternal, and labor organizations will provide in terms of financial assistance for out-of-town family travel, food for funeral attendees following the burial, etc.

   f. Notify CONCERNS OF POLICE SURVIVORS (C.O.P.S.) tx (301) 599-0445. Members are available to provide emotional support to surviving families.

   g. Carry a pager at all times.

   h. Act as a long-term liaison with the surviving family who ensures that close contact with the survivors and additional support is provided at these times.

i. If no court proceedings surround the circumstances of the officer's death, the FAMILY LIAISON OFFICER will relay all details of the incident to the family at the earliest opportunity.

j. If criminal violations surround the death, the FAMILY LIAISON OFFICER will:

   i. Inform the family of all new developments prior to press release;

   ii. Keep the family apprised of legal and parole proceedings.

   iii. Introduce the family to victim assistance specialists of the court;

   iv. Encourage the family to attend the trial and accompany them whenever possible; and

   v. Arrange for investigators to meet with the family at the earliest opportunity following the trial to answer all their questions.

D. DEPARTMENT LIAISON OFFICER

1. This position is normally assigned to a Department supervisor because of the need to effectively coordinate resources throughout the Department.

2. DEPARTMENT LIAISON OFFICER responsibilities:

   a. Work closely with the FAMILY LIAISON OFFICER and the Department chaplain to ensure that the needs of the family are fulfilled.

   b. Handle the news media throughout the ordeal. If the family decides to accept an interview, an officer should attend to "screen" questions presented to the family so as not to jeopardize subsequent legal proceedings.

   c. Meet with the following persons to coordinate funeral activities and establish an itinerary:

    i. Chief of Police and supervisors

    ii. Funeral Director

    iii. Family clergy person

    iv. Department chaplain(s)

    v. Cemetery Director

    vi. Honor Guard

d. Direct the funeral activities of the Department and visiting police departments according to the wishes of the family.

e. Issue a teletype message to Michigan area and surrounding departments and include the following:

    i. Name of deceased;

    ii. Date and time of death;

    iii. Circumstances surrounding the death;

    iv. Funeral arrangements (state if service will be private or a police funeral);

    v. Uniform to be worn;

    vi. Expressions of sympathy in lieu of flowers;

    vii. Contact person and phone number for visiting departments to indicate their desire to attend and to obtain further information.

f. Obtain an American flag from the American Legion. If the family wishes a flag presentation by the Chief of Police, notify the Chief's office.

g. If the family desires a burial in uniform, select an officer to obtain a uniform and all accouterments (except weapons) and deliver them to the funeral home.

h. Assign officers for usher duty at the church.

i. The Chief or a representative will deliver the officer's personal belongings to the family.

j. Brief the Chief and staff concerning all funeral arrangements.

k. Ensure that the parents and spouse are afforded recognition and that proper placement is arranged for them during the funeral and procession.

l. Arrange for a standby doctor for the family, if necessary.

m. Coordinate traffic management (with other jurisdictions if necessary) during the viewing, funeral, and procession. Arrange for a tow truck to be available along the procession route.

n. Assign an officer to remain at the family home during the funeral arrangements, viewing, and funeral.

o. Maintain a roster of all departments sending personnel to the funeral, including:

   i. Name and address of responding agency;

   ii. Name of the Chief of Police;

   iii. Number of officers responding;

   iv. Number of officers attending the reception after the funeral; and

   v. Number of vehicles.

p. Assist in making the necessary accommodations (food, lodging, etc.).

q. Acknowledge visiting and assisting departments.

r. Arrange for routine residence checks by the Patrol Division of the survivor's home for six (6) to eight (8) weeks following the funeral. This service is necessary since large amounts of money are passing through the residence and the survivors will be spending much time away from the home dealing with legal matters.

E. DEPARTMENT CHAPLAIN

1. The DEPARTMENT CHAPLAIN is to assist the family and his/her fellow law enforcement officers through their sadness and grief. The DEPARTMENT CHAPLAIN'S role is much broader than conducting a funeral service. The ministry begins when the DEPARTMENT CHAPLAIN is first notified of the death of a police officer and extends beyond the interment. During the funeral, the DEPARTMENT CHAPLAIN comforts the bereaved and pays tribute to the fallen officer. The DEPARTMENT CHAPLAIN serves as a counselor, pastor, and friend to the family of the deceased.

2. The DEPARTMENT CHAPLAIN has a dual role—as a member of the law enforcement community and as an ordained clergy person. The elements that the DEPARTMENT CHAPLAIN must balance are the military style ceremony and the religious rite. The military ceremony recognizes the service and sacrifice of the law enforcement officer. The religious rite extends a spiritual ministry to the family, friends, and the law enforcement community.

3. Since the conduct of the funeral service takes the wishes of the family into account, the DEPARTMENT CHAPLAIN may be asked to cooperate with the family's clergy person. Since the funeral service is primarily pastoral and properly a function of the local clergy person, the DEPARTMENT CHAPLAIN should accede to the desire of the civilian clergy person as much as possible.

4. When law enforcement personnel die of any cause, the family of the deceased must be consulted at every stage of the planning. The DEPARTMENT CHAPLAIN and the officer(s) assigned to assist the family should in no way disrupt the plans or wishes of the family and their religious clergy and advisors. The DEPARTMENT CHAPLAIN and officer(s) need to be

readily available to accommodate the planning activities associated with the funeral. Keep in mind always the degree of involvement of those assigned to assist the family are to do so at the sole prerogative of the family. All plans, as they develop, are communicated continually to the Chief of Police and other command personnel. The DEPARTMENT CHAPLAIN and officers may only be called upon in an advisory role.

If the family does not wish to have a departmental funeral, their wishes have to be honored. When a departmental funeral is not desired, a memorial service for the deceased should be considered shortly after the family's funeral for the deceased. A memorial service allows departmental personnel, area law enforcement personnel, and the community to pay their last respects to the deceased. The family should be invited to this memorial service.

F. BENEFITS COORDINATOR

1. The BENEFITS COORDINATOR will gather information on ALL benefits/funeral payments available to the family. The BENEFITS COORDINATOR has the Department's full support to fulfill this responsibility to the survivors and is completely responsible for filing the appropriate benefit paperwork and following through with the family to ensure that these benefits are being received.

2. The BENEFITS COORDINATOR is responsible for:

   a. Filing Worker's Compensation claims and related paperwork.

   b. Contacting the appropriate municipal offices without delay to ensure that the beneficiary receives death and retirement benefits, the officer's remaining paychecks, and payment for remaining annual and compensatory time.

   c. Gathering information on all benefit/funeral payments that are available to the family.

   d. Setting up any special trust funds or educational funds.

e. Notifying police organizations (such as the Fraternal Order of Police, the Police Officer's Association of Michigan, the Michigan Association or Police, etc.) of the death and to ensure that any and all entitlements are paid to the beneficiary(s). These agencies may also offer legal and financial counseling to the family at no cost.

f. Preparing a printout of the various benefits/funeral payments that are due to the family, listing named beneficiaries, contacts at various benefits offices, and when they can expect to receive payment.

g. Meeting with the surviving family a few days after the funeral to discuss the benefits they will receive. A copy of the prepared printout and any other related paperwork should be given to the family at this time.

   i. If there are surviving children from a former marriage, the guardian of those children should also receive a printout of what benefits the children may be receiving.

   ii. Attention should be given to the revocation of health benefits. The majority of health benefit providers allow a thirty-day (30) grace period before canceling or imposing monthly payments upon survivors.

h. Meeting again with the family in about six (6) months to make sure that they are receiving benefits.

VI. CONTINUED SUPPORT FOR THE FAMILY

Members of the Department must remain sensitive to the needs of the survivors long after the officer's death. The grief process has no timetable and survivors may develop a complicated grief process. More than half of the surviving spouses can be expected to develop post-traumatic stress reaction to the tragedy.

Survivors should continue to feel a part of the "police family." They should be invited to Department activities to ensure continued contact.

A. DEPARTMENTAL SUPPORT

1. Members of the Department are encouraged to keep in touch with the family. The Chaplain's Corps, co-workers, and others (officials) should arrange with the family to visit the home from time to time so long as the family expresses a desire to have these contacts continue.

2. The Chief of Police should observe the officer's death date with a short note to the family and/or flowers on the grave.

3. Holidays may be especially difficult for the family, particularly if small children are involved. Increased contact with the survivors and additional support is important at these times.

VII. FUNERAL–ACTIVE LAW ENFORCEMENT OFFICERS

A. According to the wishes of relatives of the deceased officer, the Chief of Police may designate an officer to act as officer in charge of the funeral detail. The officer in charge of the funeral shall plan the ceremony to fit the particular circumstances. The physical layout of the area where the funeral will be held, availability of a bugler or firing party, and the desires of the relatives of the deceased will result in modifications.

B. According to the wishes of the family, a deceased law enforcement officer who was on active service at the time of death may be provided with a uniform for burial. NOTE: While the officer's badges and weapons may be displayed, the hat and badge, breast badge, and weapon shall not be buried with the officer.

C. The officer in charge shall confer with the Chief of Police regarding the assignment of officers to the funeral detail and designate the uniform to be worn by all attending uniformed officers.

D. The funeral detail shall normally consist of the following uniformed officers:

1. The officer in charge designated by the Chief of Police.

2. Six (6) to eight (8) officers to act as pallbearers.

3. One (1) squad (consisting of one (1) sergeant and five (5) officers) to act as an honor guard, which may also serve as pallbearers.

E.   The officer in charge shall properly train and rehearse the entire detail to enable them to present a fitting service.

F.   The Department has a supply of gloves and mourning ribbons for funeral details. The officer in charge of the detail shall replenish the supply as needed.

G.   If the relatives wish, the officer in charge shall ensure the presence of an American and/or Michigan flag.

   1. During the time when the body is on view to the public, the flags may be folded in the proper manner and laid inside the casket or displayed near it. (See Section XI, subsections A and B—Correct Methods of Folding Flags.)

   2. After the casket is closed, the flag shall be draped over the casket. The American flag shall be draped so the star field is over the left shoulder of the deceased.

   3. Flags shall be furnished by the Department or the American Legion.

H.   The officer in charge shall confer with the funeral director to ensure coordination in the service.

I.   The officer in charge shall make a survey of the chapel or religious institution (as well as the actual grave site) to determine routes and the most desirable positions for the formation of the funeral escort.

   1. Arrangements for traffic control should also be made at this time, including (when practical) the assignment of two (2) officers to stand at attention—one on each side of the entrance to the cemetery—during the time the funeral party is entering.

J.   The officer in charge shall determine that there are sufficient reserved seats in the chapel or religious institution for the uniformed officers attending who are not taking part in the funeral ceremony. Arrangements shall also be made to have an officer escort the spouses of law enforcement officers to a group of seats reserved for them.

K.   Depending on their availability, a firing detail, bugler, and pipe and drum corps may be used. The officer in charge shall determine the availability of these services to the family of a deceased law enforcement officer.

1. When the deceased is a veteran, the officer in charge shall make appropriate arrangements with American Legion Post 51 or other veteran's organizations to obtain the services of trained personnel if the relatives desire a color guard, firing party, and a bugler.

VIII. FUNERAL–RETIRED LAW ENFORCEMENT OFFICERS

A. The same general procedures established for active law enforcement officer's funerals are followed in cases of deceased retired law enforcement officers, except only the following department services may be provided.

1. Officer in charge.

2. Department chaplain.

3. Honor guard only maintained for one (1) hour prior to the funeral service (may also serve as pallbearers).

4. Flags shall be furnished by the Department or the American Legion.

5. NOTE: Deceased retired law enforcement officers shall be furnished a uniform for burial if the family desires.

B. If additional department involvement is requested by the family, prior authorization shall be received from the Chief of Police.

IX. OFFICERS ATTENDING THE FUNERAL CEREMONY

A. HONOR GUARD

1. If the deceased was an active law enforcement officer, an honor guard may be maintained during times of viewing and on the day of the funeral. If the deceased was a retired law enforcement officer, an honor guard may be maintained for approximately one (1) hour prior to the funeral service. Whether or not

an honor guard will be maintained shall be determined by the officer in charge, taking all circumstances into consideration (including the wishes of the family). In any event, a member of the department shall be present to assist relatives and friends calling to pay their respects.

2. An honor guard consists of two (2) officers wearing white gloves, standing at attention and covered, one at the head and one at the foot of the casket during the hours that the body is on view to the public. A military honor guard shall be maintained at the casket in the chapel or religious institution for an hour or more (as the occasion demands) immediately before the funeral service commences. The honor guard shall be changed every ten (10) to fifteen (15) minutes to provide relief. This guard is removed when a prearranged signal is given by the funeral director as the chaplain is about to start the service. The honor guard shall then take seats with the funeral escort detail, unless they are also acting as pallbearers.

3. The honor guard shall consist of one (1) squad, including one (1) sergeant and five (5) officers.

4. The honor guard shall be changed in the following manner. Originally, one (1) officer shall march to the head of the casket and the other to the foot. Then, in unison, they execute an "about face." When this maneuver has been executed, they should then be in position at the head and foot of the casket. It may, however, be necessary at times to slightly vary this procedure because of conditions.

B. PALLBEARERS

1. The Pallbearers shall wear white gloves at all times and shall remain covered while actually carrying the casket, which is carried feet first. At the proper time, two (2) pallbearers previously designated shall remove the flag and fold it in the proper manner. (See Section X, subsection B– Graveside Ceremony). (See Section XI, subsections A and B–Correct Methods of Folding Flags.) The flag shall then be passed to the Chief of Police, or in his/her absence, the ranking officer present, who presents it to the nearest of kin.

2. If the family of the deceased wishes to use non-department pall-bearers, the designated officer may act as honorary pallbearer.

3. If the family requests to have officers other than those assigned to the detail to act as pallbearers, they shall be advised that the requested officers shall act as honorary pallbearers.

C. OTHER OFFICERS ATTENDING THE FUNERAL CEREMONY

1. To ease the planning by the officer in charge and the funeral director, officers planning to attend in uniform in an individual capacity shall notify the officer in charge on arrival for instructions.

2. When uniformed officers walk by the casket to pay their respects, or as they enter the home, chapel, or religious institution, they shall carry their cover over the left breast and remain uncovered during the ceremony.

D. FUNERAL ESCORT

1. The funeral escort shall be placed in formation along the path the casket is carried from the home, chapel, or religious institution to the hearse. Modifications in placing this formation will vary with conditions present. Ordinarily, a rank of officers is formed on each side of the path. When conditions do not permit this, the officers may be in a military formation nearby, or if the size of the escort is large, a combination of both plans may be followed.

   a. Procession from chapel or religious institution to the hearse shall be as follows:

      i. Escort.

      ii. Clergyperson(s).

      iii. Pallbearers and honorary pallbearers.

      iv. Casket.

v. Family.

vi. Department officers.

vii. Other police officers.

viii. Distinguished persons, delegations and societies, and other persons in attendance.

2. Uniformed department officers and representatives of other departments in uniform (if not on an assignment with the funeral escort) may be in a formation behind the escort detail, if desired. In this formation and during the services, uniformed officers from other departments shall be grouped according to their respective departments.

3. On the appearance of the casket, the officer in charge calls the formation to attention by command "ATTENTION." The officer in charge then calls the formation to a right-hand salute by the order "PRESENT ARMS." If the distance between the formation and the funeral escort makes this plan impractical, an officer in the formation should be designated also to give the commands on the appearance of the casket.

4. This salute shall be held until the casket has been placed inside the hearse or has entered the church or home at which time the command "ORDER ARMS" shall be given, followed by the commands necessary to order further movement of the escort as conditions demand.

5. Department law enforcement officers not in uniform shall stand at attention and hold their hand over the left breast in the above cases.

6. The formation described in paragraph two (2) above (if used) shall proceed in an orderly manner into the chapel or religious institution or to their cars.

X. FUNERAL

A. PROCESSION TO CEMETERY

1. The procession to the cemetery shall be formed as nearly as possible in the following order:

    a. All Buchanan City police/emergency vehicles not involved as escort, followed by all other law enforcement agency/ emergency vehicles.

    b. Escort vehicle(s).

    c. Funeral director/clergy person vehicle.

    d. Pallbearers and honorary pallbearers vehicle(s).

    e. Hearse.

    f. Flower carrying vehicle (if used).

    g. Family vehicle(s).

    h. Distinguished persons, delegations and societies, and other person's vehicles.

B. GRAVESIDE CEREMONY

    1. A previously designated detail shall leave the home, chapel, or religious institution far enough in advance of the funeral procession to enable them to reach the cemetery and station themselves along the path where the casket will be carried from the hearse to the grave. This will eliminate the confusion of stationing this detail after the procession arrives.

    2. In the event the color guard or firing detail is used, they shall lead and no part of the formation shall be to the right or in front of the colors.

    3. The remainder of the uniformed department officers present who are not otherwise assigned, shall immediately (on arrival) form ranks to the right of the grave. On appearance of the casket, the formation shall be brought to attention. The officer in charge and the officers forming the ranks from the hearse to the grave shall come to the right-hand salute. The balance of the formation remains at attention until the casket has been placed

on the grave. Non-uniformed officers shall stand at attention and hold their hand over the left breast. The command "ORDER ARMS" shall be given to end the salute and this shall be followed by the order "PARADE REST" for the formation. The officers in the ranks along the path of the casket shall then follow the casket to the grave and join the formation to the right of the grave.

    a. During the service at the grave, officers in formation shall remain covered.

4. Two previously designated pallbearers shall remove and fold the flag. The flag is folded immediately after the sounding of taps during a military funeral. After passing the flag to the Chief (or in his/her absence the ranking officer present), the formation is then brought to attention, given the proper orders, marched a reasonable distance from the grave, and dismissed.

    a. The United States flag and the Michigan flag (if used) are presented to the next of kin with some statement on behalf of the State, such as "This flag is (or these flags are) offered by a grateful State and Nation and in memory of the faithful service performed by your loved one."

D. OUT OF STATE BURIAL

In cases where the deceased officer's body is taken out of state for burial, arrangements shall be made by the Chief of Police for suitable escort to accompany the body, permission for out-of state travel, and any other special requirements.

XI. CORRECT METHODS OF FOLDING FLAGS

A. UNITED STATES FLAG

1. The two (2) pallbearers designated to fold the flag grasp each corner and step slightly to one side. They then fold the lower striped section of the flag over the blue field.

2. The folded edge is then folded over to meet the open edge.

3. A triangular fold is started by bringing the striped corner of the

folded edge to the open edge.

4. The outer point is turned inward, parallel with the open edge to form a second triangle.

5. The triangle folding is continued until the entire length of the flag is folded in this manner.

6. When the flag is completely folded, only the blue field shall be visible and it shall be folded in the triangular shape of a cocked hat.

B. MICHIGAN FLAG

1. The two (2) pallbearers designated to fold the flag grasp each corner and step slightly to one side. Turn the flag front side down.

2. Fold the white border edge five (5) inches inward.

3. Fold the flag lengthwise leaving the top of the State seal facing down.

4. Fold the open edge over to meet the folded edge, leaving the top of the State seal facing down.

5. At the end opposite of the white border, make a fold inward AT the near edge of the State seal.

6. Start a triangular fold at the white border end by bringing the corner of the folded edge to the open edge.

7. Turn the outer point inward parallel with the open edge is form a second triangle.

8. Continue the triangle folding until the length of the flag to folded in this manner.

9. Complete the fold by tucking the final edge into the open triangle fold.

XII. MOURNING BADGE RIBBON

A. The mourning badge ribbon is a black fabric band which (when worn) drapes law enforcement officer's uniform breast badge. This ribbon is a visual symbol of the grief felt at the loss of a fellow officer.

B. Mourning badge ribbons shall be worn by uniformed law enforcement officers of the department, according to the following:

  1. When an officer dies while on duty status, all uniformed law enforcement officers, whether attending the funeral or not, shall wear a mourning badge ribbon on the day of the funeral. The "day of the funeral" shall encompass the entire twenty-four (24) hour period of the calendar day on which the funeral is scheduled.

    a. For a duty-incurred death of a law enforcement officer, Operations shall transmit to all department LEIN locations the date the mourning badge ribbon shall be worn.

  2. Law enforcement officers in uniform <u>attending the funeral</u> of a department law enforcement officer, a retired law enforcement officer, or a law enforcement officer from another department, shall war a mourning badge ribbon.

  3. When the mourning badge ribbon is worn, it shall be placed horizontally around the breast badge between the shirt pin and badge, with the seam unexposed.

C. Each member of the department issued a uniform and badge is provided a mourning badge ribbon. There is a small supply of extra ribbons in the Chief's office.

XIII. MAINTENANCE AND DECORATION OF GRAVES OF DECEASED LAW ENFORCEMENT OFFICERS

A. An inspection of the grave site shall be made several days before Memorial Day so unusual conditions may be reported to the Department, who shall notify the next of kin.

XIV. DEATH BENEFITS

A. BADGES

The next of kin of any law enforcement officer who dies while an active officer of the department shall be presented with the officer's actual badge encased in a plastic stand.

1. If the officer is killed or dies while on duty status, the badge number shall be retired from service.

2. If the officer's death does not occur while on duty status, the badge number shall not be retired. A new badge may later be issued bearing that number.

XV. FUNERALS FOR OFFICERS OF OTHER DEPARTMENTS

The Chief of Police shall ensure appropriate department representation at funerals of active police officers of other departments within this area.

Brian Russell,
Chief of Police

Appendix B

FUNERAL CHECKLIST[39]

The Chief/Departmental Head and/or his/her designated representative shall:

❑ 1. Immediately assign a Family Liaison Planning Team, consisting of chaplains(s) and/or departmental personnel, to the family of the deceased member. (See Appendix C for a checklist, pages 107–108.)

❑ 2. Send computer message regarding death and funeral arrangements to all departments/agencies in the country.

❑ 3. Contact local state division of Homeland Security (or appropriate agency) and advise of the funeral and the large gathering of law enforcement and related personnel.

❑ 4. Arrange for black or blue badge mourning bands and/or black arm bands and building bunting (if desired).

❑ 5. Make arrangements to provide meals for the family from the time of death until the day of the funeral.

❑ 6. Prepare fallen member's remembrance bulletin or card. Send it to the printers.

❑ 7. Plan parking for visiting police and emergency vehicles on the day of the funeral.

❑ 8. Plan route to cemetery. This route could include a drive by the police headquarters, the fallen member's home, and schools in the community.

❑ 9. Arrange for a Casket Guard at the visitation and, if desired, a Color Guard for the funeral service.

❑ 10. Obtain white gloves for use by Pallbearers, Casket Guard and any others.

❑ 11. Make a list of all agencies in attendance at the visitation and funeral service for later thank you notes.

❑ 12. Obtain guest book(s) and uniformed personnel or other(s) to be in charge of the book (guest books are often provided by the funeral home).

❑ 13. Arrange drivers for the family and make sure that there are enough vehicles for the family's use.

❑ 14. Provide resource persons to meet the family's needs: meals, childcare, household chores, etc.

❑ 15. Have a uniformed member available to stay at the house for security while the family is making funeral arrangements, as well as during the visitation, the wake and the funeral.

❑ 16. Arrange for any flowers–carnations. [**Note:** the use of flowers at Jewish funerals is discouraged–check with the family's Rabbi.]

❑ 17. Arrange for pallbearers in consultation with family.

❑ 18. Arrange for ushers to assist the funeral director during the funeral service.

❑ 19. Make motel/hotel arrangements for visiting police officers.

❑ 20. Arrange for security for the visiting police and emergency vehicles, as well as assisting and parking these vehicles.

❑ 21. Provide for a funeral meal or refreshments and servers.

❑ 22. Provide for set-up personnel for the funeral meal: tables, chairs, etc.

❑ 23. Line up clean-up personnel after the meal.

❏ 24. Arrange for a bugler to play "Taps" at the conclusion of the graveside service.

❏ 25. Arrange for bagpipe(s) or pipe and drum corps (if desired). Note: one piper may be sufficient in most circumstances.

❏ 26. Arrange for a firing detail to fire blank shotgun, rifle or pistol volleys at the conclusion of the graveside service.

❏ 27. Have an Honor Guard in front of the fallen member's home and headquarters from the time of death through the funeral service and meal.

❏ 28. Arrange for the police station/post, city/government flags to be flown at half-staff.

❏ 29. Arrange for national or state flag as a casket cover for presentation to the family. (Make sure the pallbearers know how to fold the flag.)

❏ 30. If the burial of the deceased member is to be out-of-state or the region, arrange for a suitable escort to the grave site and contact a local law enforcement agency to arrange a graveside committal service.

Appendix C

FAMILY LIAISON PLANNING TEAM
CHECKLIST OF FAMILY NEEDS

Deceased members full name: _____

When did they join the department?: _____

Is a photograph of the member available? _____ Yes _____ No
    A photograph in uniform? _____ Yes _____ No

Family members' names: Relationship to the deceased:

_____   _____

_____   _____

_____   _____

_____   _____

_____   _____

_____   _____

Are there other family members that need to be notified?

Name: _____ Contact information: _____

Name: _____ Contact information: _____

Name: _____ Contact information: _____

Name: _____ Contact information: _____

107

Is childcare needed for the family? _____ Yes _____ No

Does the family have a funeral home preference?: _____

    Address: _____ Telephone: _____

Family preferred funeral service and burial date and time?:_____

    Note: Because of the distance that law enforcement personnel from surround-
    ing communities and states will need to travel, it is suggested that a
    Tuesday, Wednesday, Thursday, or Friday would be the best day. A mid-
    morning beginning for the service is preferable.

The deceased/family's religious preference?: _____

Whom would the family like to have officiate at the funeral service?:

Name: _____ Title:_____

Address: _____

Telephone numbers:_____ _____ _____
                         Office   Home   Cellular/Pager

    Note: If the family has no preference, offer the services of a law enforcement
    chaplain. If your department has no chaplain, contact the International
    Conference of Police Chaplains for assistance in finding an area chaplain
    for your use: 850-654-9736.

Will the family allow a military style funeral service?: _____ Yes _____ No

    Note: You may need to explain the reason a military style service is preferred.

Does the family have a preference as to whom the pallbearers that carry the casket
will be?:

Was the deceased a member of the military?: _____ Yes _____ No

    Military branch: _____

    Do they wish a military presence at the service?: _____ Yes _____ No

Assist the family in beginning to develop an obituary for the funeral announcement.

Appendix D

FOR A CIVILIAN RELIGIOUS OFFICIANT

Dear Religious Officiant:

The family of a law enforcement officer that has been killed in the line-of-duty has asked you to be involved in a burial service for their loved one. If plans for the funeral service have not been made, you will need to be directly involved in this planning. Families are numb with grief and cannot think coherently for a few hours after receiving the news. You will need to use discretion as to when funeral plans are to be discussed. Up to six hours may be necessary before actual planning begins. However, you will need to inform the family of planning that is considered urgent. High on that agenda is a determination as to whether or not the family wishes to speak to the media. If not, then is there a relative or family friend they wish to designate as their spokesperson? If this is not possible, then the media will be notified that "The family has no comment at this time. All information regarding the family, funeral, etc. will come from the department's or agency's media relations office."

A line-of-duty death was the result of an on-duty situation that took the officer's life. This may have been a vehicular accident, felonious assault, or any circumstance that led to the officer's death. The below material is offered to assist you in this overwhelming responsibility. The law enforcement officer's department or agency has or will likely assign an officer or a chaplain, or both to work with you. Although you have been involved in burial services before, you may not be ready for the style and size of this service.

Size of the service: This service will likely be larger than any other service you have done before. You can expect up to two thousand uniformed law enforcement officers, fire fighters and emergency responders to be in attendance. Then there may be civilian political leaders. All these are in addition to the family and friends. The site where the service will be conducted will need to seat at least two thousand persons, possibly more. The funeral procession from the place of service to the burial site may be several miles long.

Style of the service: Law enforcement communities are paramilitary organizations. Therefore, law enforcement burial services, especially a line-of-duty death, are usually based on military tradition. This will involve uniformed personnel in military procession and recession. Officers from the larger law enforcement community will want to pay their respects to a deceased brother or sister even if they personally didn't know the officer. There will be an honor guard made up of members of the officer's department, or in the case of a smaller department, officers from surrounding police agencies. In honor of the officer's life and service, this honor guard will be assigned to the officer's remains from shortly after his or her death until the casket is lowered into the ground and is covered with soil. This would include an officer's cremains. If the family wishes not to bury the cremains, an officer would accompany the remains to the family home or to where they are to remain. If the family wishes some private time with their loved ones, the honor guard can be requested to leave the room during this time. The procession past the casket, prior to the beginning of the service or at the conclusion of the service, may take an hour or more. The visual show of respect by the law enforcement community can be a real sense of assurance for the grieving family members. The grave site service usually involves a military style of burial with a firing detail and bugle(s) and may involve a pipe and drum corps. The officer will likely be buried in uniform. As a sign of respect for the deceased officer, flags are usually flown at half-staff. The law enforcement officers will also likely place a narrow black or dark blue ribbon across their badges to show their solidarity and respect.

Suggested day of the week and time for the service: Because of the distance that law enforcement personnel from surrounding communities and states will need to travel, it is suggested that a Tuesday, Wednesday, Thursday, or Friday would be the best day. A midmorning beginning for the service is preferable.

Note: If the family wishes to have a private service before such a large, military style service, a smaller service could be offered the day before. This additional service can be offered, but it will wear on the family.

Also, note: If the family does not wish to have a military style service, the department/agency will honor this request. But because of the nature of a line-of-duty death, the law enforcement and local communities will need to pay their respect to their deceased sister or brother. After the family's service, a memorial service will likely be created to meet these needs. This service serves as a way to show respect and gain some closure to this tragic event. The family would be invited to the memorial service. The department/agency could invite you to be a part of this service.

A word of warning: Word spreads quickly about a line-of-duty death. The media arrives on the scene of the death shortly after a tragedy occurs. The media follows the body of the officer to the hospital, to the funeral home, to the service, and to the grave site service. The media may contact you personally about more information. It is strongly suggested that you <u>do not</u> respond to their request for information but, rather, refer them back to the law enforcement officer's department or agency for the latest information.

Signed: _____
Agency contact information

Appendix E

PERSONNEL DEBRIEFINGS

It is important that departmental personnel are debriefed following a line of duty death or an off duty death. Examples of debriefing models are CISD/CISM and NOVA (see "Personnel Debriefing," page 67).

Debriefings are strongly recommended for:

1. Personnel involved in the event (e.g., those fired at, injured, those who fired rounds during the event).

2. Personnel who were partners, or who responded to the event (including personnel from other departments/agencies, evidence technicians, departmental chaplains, on-duty dispatch personnel, ambulance/EMT personnel, hospital emergency/operating room personnel), and those who witnessed the event.

3. Personnel involved in the death notification.

4. Personnel on the same shifts or from a shift that recently went off duty. This could include all shifts, dispatch and civilian personnel of the agency.

   [**Note:** Debriefing of the chief and supervisory personnel should take place separately. Also, Chaplains who responded to the scene should be debriefed and **NOT** be debriefers.]

5. Other debriefings that should be encouraged:
   A. Other law enforcement personnel from other departments.
   B. Personal friends of the officer killed.
   C. Honor Guards/Color Guards.

113

   D. Other spouses/partners (especially line of duty deaths).
   E. Chaplain Corps
   F. City/town/township supervisors, mayors, etc.

ENDNOTES

1. "In Person, In Time." Manual prepared in cooperation with: Dr. Thomas L. Bennett, State Medical Examiner, the Iowa Organization for Victim Assistance (IOVA), MADD/Polk County Chapter, and Polk County Victim Services. Crime Victim Assistance Division, Iowa Department of Justice, Thomas J. Miller, Attorney General of Iowa. A copy may be obtained from Crime Victim Assistance Division, Old Historical Building, Des Moines, Iowa 50319, (515) 281-5044 or (800) 373-5044.

2. Droge, Arthur J. An excellent overview of Christianity's development of its negative view toward suicide can be found in Droge's article "Did Paul commit suicide?", *Bible Review* Vol. V, No. 6, December, 1989, pp. 14–21, 42.

3. American Legion. National Americanism Commission. *Let's be Right on Flag Etiquette.* Indianapolis, Indiana, rev. May, 1996, p. 15. Quoting from: The United States Flag Code (Title 36, Chap. 10, paragraphs 170–178).

4. Based on funeral arrangements suggested by the Rockford Police Department, Rockford, Illinois; and, W. Troy McClain, Vince J. Aurentz and Harvey L. Ellis' article, "Police Funeral Coordination Team." *Law and Order*, September 1983, p. 78.

5. Christensen, James L. *Funeral Services for Today.* Old Tappan, New Jersey: Fleming H. Revell Company, 1977, p. 42, invocational prayer adapted from.

6. The American Legion, *The American Legion Post Commander's Guide and Manual of Ceremonies.* Indianapolis, Indiana, 1969, pp. 76–77, pastoral prayer adapted from.

7. Reardon, James P., compiler. *Conducting and Managing Fire Service Funerals and Ceremonies.* Albion, Michigan: The Western Michigan Fire Chiefs Association, 1983, p. 58, pastoral prayer adapted from.

8. Christensen, op. cit., pp. 46–47, 89–90, meditation example adapted from.

9. Stamm, Sister Ann, D.Min., author. Chaplain with the Livonia Police Department, Livonia, Michigan.

10. Ibid.

11. Crowther, J. Nevin, author, Chaplain with the Ramsey County Sheriff's Department, Minnesota. Invocation prayer adapted from "The Chaplain's Message–Bud," February 5, 1994.

12. International Commission on English in the Liturgy. *The Roman Ritual, Shorter Book of Blessings,* New York: Catholic Book Publishing Company, 1990: p. 320.

13. Habig, Marion A., edited by. *St. Francis of Assisi. Writings and Early Biographies, English Omnibus of the Sources for the Life of St. Francis.* Chicago: Franciscan Herald Press, p. 127.
14. Author of shortened version unknown. Original *Tribute to a Dog* was written by Senator George Vest in 1870.
15. Charles Dickerson, retired Chief of Police, Edgewood Police Dept., Kentucky.
16. From a plaque hanging in the Canine Training Unit Headquarters of the St. Paul Police Department, St. Paul, Minnesota.
17. A reading adapted from reflection given for K-9 "Dick" by Chaplain Norman J. Green, Burbank Police Department, Burbank, California, December 8, 1992.
18. Crowther, loc. cit., meditation adapted.
19. Popish, Minnie Boyd, author. "Pets" from *The Symphony of Life from the Salesian Collection*, Sara Tarascio, compiler, New Rochelle, New York: Salesian Inspirational Books, 1994: p. 110.
20. Edwards, Inez, author, "A Tribute to Fallen Officer Brett Sumner," Cedar Rapids Police Department, Cedar Rapids, Iowa. The poem was written for Officer Sumner's funeral and read by Sgt. Scott Phillips. The poem was adapted slightly.
21. Gothery, Officer Thomas, author, The American Police Hall of Fame, North Port, Florida 33596.
22. Koch, Detective Harry, author, retired, Maricopa County Sheriff's Office, Arizona.
23. Robertson, Chaplain Tommy, author, Van Zandt Sheriff's Department, Texas.
24. Jordan, John and Reetika Vazirani, lyrics. Music: *Amazing Grace* by John Newton, 1725–1807. Tune: "AMAZING GRACE CM." Copies of lyrics, sheet music, and a vocal rendition on audio cassette may be ordered from the National Law Enforcement Officer's Memorial Fund, (800) 331-5171 or (301) 340-1600, FAX (301) 251-5887.
25. Park, Chaplain Carol, Detroit Police Department, Detroit, Michigan, lyrics.
26. Stamm, loc. cit.
27. Calkin, Ruth Harms, author. From *Life's Little Prayer Book,* Gary Lahoda, compiler, Baltimore: Ottenheimer Publishers, Inc., #165.
28. Augustine, author. From John Beilenson, compiler. *Prayers for Inner Strength,* White Plains, New York: Peter Pauper Press, 1986.
29. Baillie, John, author. From Frederick B. Macnutt, compiler, *The Prayer Manual,* A. R. Mowbray and Company, Ltd., 1961.
30. Andrews, Lancelot, author. Macnutt, loc. cit.
31. Mohammed, from the Qur'an.
32. Surah of Jonah, v. 57. Cragg, Kenneth, compiler. *Alive to God, Muslim and Christian Prayer*, London: Oxford University Press, 1970: p. 153.
33. Jomier, Jacques. *How to Understand Islam,* New York: The Crossroad Publishing Company, 1991: p. 58.
34. From William W. Simpson. *Jewish Prayer and Worship, an Introduction for Christians*, New York: Seabury Press, 1967, p. 97.
35. Ibid., p. 98.

36. Hertz, Joseph H., ed. *Authorized Daily Prayer Book*, New York: Block Publishing Company, 1955: p. 212.
37. Erickson, Laurie A., notes from a lecture given at the Michigan State Police Academy, October 8, 1999. Mrs. Erickson is the surviving wife of Michigan State Trooper, Byron J. Erickson, who died in the line of duty on July 31, 1993. Mrs. Erickson can be a resource to agencies/departments.
38. Erickson, ibid.
39. Funeral checklist based on list from Rockford Police Department, Rockford, Illinois.

INDEX

A

Agencies, support helps and survivor resources, 66–68
Anglican funeral information, 13
Animal memorial service:
    Burial site, 44
    Introductory statement, 39
    Line-of-duty death, 39–44
    Off-duty or retired, 44
    Rationale, 39
    Rifle/pistol/shotgun volley, 44
    Taps, 44
Arm bands, mourning, 19, 25, 103
Attorneys, 21, 26

B

Badge, mourning bands, 19, 25, 103
Bagpipes, 17, 33, 105
Bagpipes, prerecorded, 22
Benefits, Public Safety Officer's, 63, 68,
Bereavement resources, 66–67
Buddhist funeral information, 11–12
Bugler, 17, 105
Bulletin, remembrance or card, 22, 103
Bunting, building, 25, 103
Burial, out-of-state/region, 26, 105

C

Card, remembrance or bulletin, 22, 103
Caring for the deceased member's family, 62–65
Casket, drape with flag, 18, 23, 105
Casket guard, 17, 23–24, 104
Catholic (Roman) funeral information, 13

Cemetery formation, 33
Chaplain, police:
    Dual role, 7–8
    Role of, 7–8
    Military salute, 8
    Uniform, 8
Checklist, funeral, 103–105
Child care for family, 25
Children of the deceased member, emotional support of, 64–65
CISD/CISM (Critical Incident Stress Debriefing/Management), 67
Civilian religious officiant information, 109–111
Clergy religious garment, 8
Color Guard, 17, 33, 104
Contributions, memorial, 26
Court proceedings, 25

D

Death benefits, 63, 68
Death notifications, 5–7, 14–15
Debriefings, personnel, 67, 113–114
Dog, Memorial service:
    Introductory statement, 39
    Line-of-duty death, 39–44
    Off-duty or retired death, 44
    Rationale, 39
Drum and pipe corps, 17, 33, 105

F

Family:
    Benefits, 63, 68
    Chauffeur-driven, for family, 24
    Child care, 25

Death benefits, member, 63, 68
Faith representative (clergy), family's, 109–111
Criminal court proceedings, 25
Hospital visitation, 14
Insurance benefits, 63, 68
Legal advisor, 25
Meals, 11–12, 25, 103, 104
"Promoting healthy healing," 62–65
Security for their home during arrangements, visitation, funeral, 25–26, 104
"Taking care of our own," 61–62
Transportation, 25
Video, create, 65
Family liaison planning team, 13–14, 103, 107–108
Firing detail, 18, 105
Flag, American:
    Etiquette, 18–19
    Draping of the casket, 23, 105
    Displaying:
        In building, 19
        Across a street, 19
    Folding, 23, 99–100
    Half-staff, 18, 105
    Other countries, 18
Flag presentation, 19, 105
Flowers, 19, 104
Flowers at Jewish funerals (use discouraged), 12, 64, 104
Funeral home director, 21, 104
Funeral meal, 12, 64, 104
Funeral procession to cemetery, 24, 103
Funeral service:
    Animal memorial service, 39–44
    Arrangements, 20–26
    Bag pipes, 17, 33, 105
    Casket Guard, 17, 23, 105
    Checklist, 103–105
    Faith leader, non-police, 109–111
    Flag, 18, 23, 105
    Flower carrying vehicle, 24, 33
    Honor guard, 17–18, 26, 63, 105
    Hymns, police, 52–53
    Inclusive, 11
    Line-of-duty death, 79–102
    Media and press, 22, 25
    Meditation example, 31–33

Off-duty, active member, 34
Out of state, 26
Pallbearers, 17–18, 23, 34, 104, 105
Parking, police vehicles, 103
Poems, short readings, 47–53
Prayers, 53–57
Press and media, 24, 25
Procession route, 24, 33, 103
Procession to cemetery, 24, 33–34, 103
Retired member, 34–35
Security, 25–26, 104
Tow Truck, 24
Ushers, 104
Funeral supply kit, 76

G

Graveside, American flag folding, 23, 99–100
Guest book, 104

H

Healthy healing for family, 62–65
Hindu funeral information, 12
Home, security, 25–26, 104
Honor guard, 17–18, 26, 63, 105
Horse memorial service:
    Introductory statement, 39
    Line-of-duty death, 39–44
    Off-duty or retired death, 44
    Rationale, 39
Horse, riderless, at cemetery, 33
Hospital visitation, family, 14
Housing for visiting departments, 24, 104
Hymns, police, 52–53

I

Islamic (Muslim) funerals:
    Funeral information, 12
    Prayers, 55

J

Jewish funerals:
    Flowers note, 64, 104
    Funeral information, 12–13
    Prayers, 56–57
    Stone left at grave site, 65

K

K–9, Dog memorial service:
   A rationale, 39
   Line of duty death, 39–44
   Off-duty or retired death, 44

L

Legal advisor/representative, 21, 25
Line of duty death:
   Animal memorial service, 39–44
   Line of duty injury or death information
      form, 71–76
   Member, 29–36
Line of duty death policy, 79–102
Lutheran funeral information, 13

M

Meal cleanup and servers, 104
Meal for visiting law enforcement personnel,
   24–25, 104
Media, print and video, 22, 25
Memorial ceremonies, 64
Memorial contributions, 26
Memorial service for departmental animal:
   Poems, short readings, animal memorial,
      40–45
   Prayers for animal memorial, 40, 44
   Service, 39–44
Memorial service in lieu of funeral service,
   13–14
Mourning:
   Arm bands, 19, 25, 103
   Badge bands, 19, 25, 103
   Building bunting, 25
   Pin-on metal ribbons, 20
   Ribbons, 20
Muslim (Islamic):
   Funeral information, 12
   Prayers, 55

N

National police week, attendance at, 64
NOVA (National Organization of Victim
   Association), 67

O

Ongoing care of family, 62–65
Orthodox (Christian) funeral information, 13
Out-of-state/region burials, 26

P

Pallbearers, 17–18, 23, 34, 104, 105
Pallbearers, honorary, 34
Personnel debriefings, 67
Pipe and drum corps, 17, 33, 105
Pin-on metal ribbons, mourning, 20
Pistol/rifle/shotgun volley, 18, 33
Pistol/rifle/shotgun volley, animal memorial,
   44
Planning team, family liaison, 13–14, 103,
   107–108
Poems, additional funeral, 47–51
Police hymns, 52–53
Policy sample, line of duty death, 79–102
Prayers, additional funeral, 53–57
Print and video media, 22, 25
Procession to cemetery, 24, 33–34, 103
"Promoting healthy healing" for deceased
   member's family, 62–65

R

Readings, additional funeral, 47–53
Religious garment, 8
Remembrance bulletin/card, 22, 103
Resource persons needed, 25
Retired animal memorial, 44
Retired member, funeral, 34–36
Ribbons at funeral, 20
Riderless horse at graveside service, 33
Rifle/pistol/shotgun volley, 18, 33
Rifle/pistol/shotgun volley, animal memorial
   service, 44
Roman Catholic funeral information, 13

S

Salute, military hand, 8
Security:
   During visitation, visitation and funeral
      services, 25–26, 104

For police and emergency vehicles, 25–26, 104
Short readings, additional funeral, 47–51
Shotgun/rifle/pistol volley, 18, 33
Shotgun/rifle/pistol volley, animal memorial service, 44
Standard Operating Procedure, line of duty death, 79–102
Suicide of a law enforcement member, 14–15, 67
Suicide special note, 16
Suicide support agencies, 67
Support agencies, 66
Support of deceased member's family, 66–68
Survivor resources, helps and support agencies, 66–67

T

"Taking care of our own"–care of deceased member's family, 61–62
Taps, 24, 105
Taps at animal memorial service, 44

Thank you notes for visiting police agencies, 22, 104
Tow truck, funeral procession, 24
Trial of suspect accused of killing member, 25
Trust fund, officer's children, 62

U

Uniforms, chaplain, 8
United States Flag Code, 18–19
Ushers, 104

V

Video and print media, 24, 25
Visitation, hospital by family, 14

W

Wake, 22–23
White gloves, pallbearers and honor guard, 76, 104

Charles C Thomas
PUBLISHER • LTD.

P.O. Box 19265
Springfield, IL 62794-9265

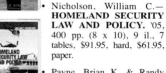

5 easy ways to order!

PHONE:
1-800-258-8980
or (217) 789-8980

FAX:
(217) 789-9130

EMAIL:
books@ccthomas.com
Web: www.ccthomas.com

MAIL:
Charles C Thomas •
Publisher, Ltd.
P.O. Box 19265
Springfield, IL 62794-9265

Complete catalog available at ccthomas.com • books@ccthomas.com

Books sent on approval • Shipping charges: $7.50 min. U.S. / Outside U.S., actual shipping fees will be charged • Prices subject to change without notice

Savings include all titles shown here and on our web site. For a limited time only.